CALIFORNIA'S SPANISH MISSIONS

Their Yesterdays and Todays

Books by Spencer Crump:

Ride the Big Red Cars
How Trolleys Helped Build Southern California

California's Spanish Missions

Redwoods, Iron Horses, and the Pacific
The Story of the California Western "Skunk" Railroad

Black Riot in Los Angeles

Henry Huntington and the Pacific Electric

Western Pacific

Rail Car, Locomotive, and Trolley Builders
An All-Time Directory

The Fundamentals of Journalism

CALIFORNIA'S SPANISH MISSIONS

Their Yesterdays and Todays

by Spencer Crump

*With Illustrations from Historical Archives,
Supplemented by Modern Photographs*

TRANS - ANGLO BOOKS

Library of Congress Cataloging in Publication Data

Crump, Spencer.
    California's Spanish missions.

    Bibliography: p. 8
    Includes index.
    1. Spanish missions of California. 2. Indians of
North America--California--Missions. 3. California--
History--To 1846. I. Title.
F864.C93   266'.2'794   73-88320
ISBN 0-87046-028-5

CALIFORNIA'S
SPANISH MISSIONS

An Album of
Their Yesterdays and Todays

by SPENCER CRUMP

Copyright © MCMLXXV
by Trans-Anglo Books

FIRST EDITION

Library of Congress Catalog Card Number: 73-88320

ISBN: 0-87046-028-5

Uncredited modern-day photographs in this book
were taken by Victoria Crump and John Crump.
Other illustrations are credited to the individuals or
organizations who made them available.

Frontispiece: The Arcade at Mission San Miguel
Endsheets: Mission Santa Barbara

BOOK DESIGN: HANK JOHNSTON

Printed and Bound in the United States of America

Published by Trans-Anglo Books,
P. O. Box 38, Corona del Mar, California 92625

Contents

•

The Missions

(From South to North)

oregon

THE COUNTIES OF CALIFORNIA

DEL NORTE

SISKIYOU

MODOC

HUMBOLDT

TRINITY

SHASTA

LASSEN

TEHAMA

PLUMAS

MENDOCINO

GLENN

BUTTE

SIERRA

COLUSA

YUBA

NEVADA

LAKE

SUTTER

PLACER

SONOMA

YOLO

EL DORADO

NAPA

ALPINE

SAN FRANCISCO SOLANO

SOLANO

SACRAMENTO

AMADOR

CALAVERAS

MARIN

SAN RAFAEL

CONTRA COSTA

SAN JOAQUIN

TUOLUMNE

MONO

SAN FRANCISCO

ALAMEDA

SAN FRANCISCO

STANISLAUS

MARIPOSA

SAN MATEO

SAN MATEO

SANTA CLARA

SANTA CLARA

SAN JOSE

MERCED

MADERA

SANTA CRUZ

SANTA CRUZ

SAN JUAN BAUTISTA

SAN BENITO

CARMEL

FRESNO

SOLEDAD

MONTEREY

INYO

PACIFIC

SAN ANTONIO

TULARE

KINGS

SAN MIGUEL

SAN LUIS OBISPO

KERN

OCEAN

SAN LUIS OBISPO

PURISIMA

SANTA INES

SAN BERNARDINO

SANTA BARBARA

SANTA BARBARA

VENTURA

LOS ANGELES

SAN BUENAVENTURA

SAN FERNANDO

SAN GABRIEL

RIVERSIDE

ORANGE

SAN JUAN CAPISTRANO

SAN LUIS REY

SAN DIEGO

IMPERIAL

SAN DIEGO

nevada

arizona

mexico

This oil painting by Jessie Person Crump depicts Santa Barbara, among the most spectacular in the mission chain.

Introduction

People with a variety of interests long have been fascinated by California's Spanish missions. For the state's residents and its visitors, they present an introduction to California's past and recall an era of pastoral beauty unmarred by "progress" represented by industry, mile-upon-mile of monotonous subdivisions, freeways, and exploitation of natural resources. To artists, they offer opportunities for creativity. For architects, the missions have inspired design themes which add beauty to homes and public buildings. Historians find them a vital part of their studies. To Catholics, they have become a symbol of faith; for those of other religions, they are examples of the fervor that the mission padres imparted to the Indians.

Lengthy volumes have been written — and still are being produced as research reveals more information — on each of these areas of interest. Many of these books are worthy of the time and study for the person with specialized interests.

This book is a study outlining why and how the missions were built, their roles in California during the Spanish and Mexican periods, and how they function today. Illustrations have been used generously to help show the nature of missions and of mission life yesterday and today.

The first section discusses the background for establishing the missions, constructing the buildings, how the Indians worked and lived at the outposts, and how the missions declined and eventually were restored. The second section is devoted to details relating to the individual missions then and now.

Appreciation for assistance in gathering material for this book is expressed to many individuals and organizations. Among those who assisted are Victor Plukas, historian for Security Pacific National Bank; Clyde Simpson, the bank's former historian; Merrilee Gwerder, director of the Wells Fargo Bank History Room; Mrs. Miriam Williams of the California State Library; Lee Burtis, librarian for the California Historical Society; James deT. Abajian, formerly with the Society, and Alan R. McElwain, formerly public relations director for the Southern California Visitors Bureau (previously known as the All-Year Club).

I am particularly grateful to the Rev. Father Maynard Geiger, O.F.M., Ph.D., who has been historian and archivist at Mission Santa Barbara for nearly forty years. Father Geiger graciously critiqued a rough draft of the manuscript for this book, clarifying factual errors and directing my attention to important areas that I had not approached. I must emphasize that Father Geiger did not edit the manuscript nor does the book incorporate his doctorinal religious views. His suggestions were in the area of historical *facts* rather than the *interpretation* of history.

Father Geiger questioned how a subject so extensive as the missions could be incorporated into a relatively compact volume such as this one: he pointed out that his files include 75,000 pages of notes alone on the subject of California missions. His two volume work on the life of Father Serra covers nearly a thousand pages.

He agreed that most people, however, read of the missions in condensed form.

The purpose of this book is to present an account in a format that will translate the mission era to the general public accurately, and without the biases of Catholicism or anti-Catholicism.

A selected bibliography is provided for those who wish to read in depth regarding the mission era. It purposely excludes most of the booklets on individual missions so that space can be devoted to the broader works covering the system.

In addition to those previously mentioned, I wish to express my appreciation to the following:

Hank Johnston, an author himself and consultant to both Trans-Anglo Books and the Flying Spur Press, who made many suggestions.

Ms. Ludmila Montoya, whose expertise in anthropology helped to provide depth.

My mother, Mrs. Jessie Person Crump, whose oil painting of Mission Santa Barbara appears in the book.

My son and daughter, John and Victoria, whose photographs of the missions today also appear in the book.

The staffs of the San Francisco, San Jose, Oakland, and Los Angeles Public Libraries; the Bancroft Library at the University of California, Berkeley; and the staffs of the libraries at the University of California, Los Angeles; University of Southern California; California State University, Fullerton, and Orange Coast College, Costa Mesa.

SPENCER CRUMP
Monterey

BIBLIOGRAPHY

Ainsworth, Katherine and Edward M., *In the Shade of the Junipero Tree: A Life of Fray Junipero Serra.* Garden City, N. Y.: Doubleday and Co., 1970.

Baer, Kurt, *Architecture of the California Missions.* Berkeley: University of California Press, 1958.

Bancroft, Hubert Howe, *California Inter Pocula.* San Francisco: The History Company, Publishers, 1888.

———, *California Pastoral, 1769-1848.* San Francisco: The History Company, Publishers, 1888.

———, *History of California,* Volumes I, II, and III. San Francisco, The History Company, Publishers, 1886.

Berger, John A., *The Franciscan Missions of California.* New York: G. P. Putnam's Sons, 1941.

Bolton, Herbert Eugene, *Anza's California Expeditions,* 5 volumes. Berkeley: University of California Press, 1930.

———, *Fray Juan Crespi, Missionary Explorer on the Pacific Coast 1769-1774.* Berkeley: University of California Press, 1927.

———, *Palou's Historical Memoirs of New California,* 4 volumes. Berkeley: University of California Press, 1926.

Bryant, Edwin, *What I Saw In California.* London: Richard Bentley, 1849.

Chapman, Charles E., *A History of California: The Spanish Period.* New York: The Macmillan Company, 1921.

Cook, Sherburne Friend, *The Conflict Between the California Indians and White Civilization.* Berkeley: University of California Press, 1943.

Corle, Edwin, *The Royal Highway.* Indianapolis: The Bobbs-Merrill Company, 1949.

Correia, Delia Richards, *Lasuen in California.* Berkeley: University of California Press, 1934.

Dana, Richard Henry, Jr., *Two Years Before the Mast.* Cleveland: The World Publishing Co., 1946.

Dutton, Davis (editor), *Missions of California.* New York: Ballentine Books, 1972.

Engelhardt, Rev. Zephyrin, O.F.M., *The Franciscans*

in California. Harbor Springs, Michigan: Holy Childhood Indian School, 1897.

————, *The Missions and Missionaries of California*. San Francisco: The James H. Barry Company, 1909.

Geary, Gerald Joseph, *The Secularization of the California Missions, 1810-1846*. Washington, D.C., Catholic University of America, 1934.

Geiger, Maynard J., O.F.M., Ph.D., *The Life and Times of Fray Junipero Serra, O.F.M., or The Man Who Never Turned Back, 1713-1784*, 2 volumes. Washington, D.C.: Academy of American Franciscan History, 1959.

————, (editor and translator), *Palou's Life of Fray Junipero Serra*. Washington, D.C.: Academy of American Franciscan History, 1955.

Gordon, Dudley, *Junipero Serra: California's First Citizen*. Los Angeles: Cultural Assets Press, 1969.

Jackson, Helen Hunt, *Father Junipero and the Mission Indians of California*. Boston: Little, Brown & Company, 1902.

————, *Glimpses of California and the Missions*. Boston: Little, Brown & Company, 1902.

————, *Ramona*, Boston: Little, Brown & Company, 1920.

James, George Wharton, *In and Out of the Old Missions of California: An Historical and Pictorial Account of the Franciscan Missions*. Boston: Little, Brown & Company, 1905.

————, *Old Missions and Mission Indians of California*. Los Angeles: B. R. Baumgardt, 1895.

Johnson, Paul (supervising editor), *The California Missions, A Pictorial History*. Menlo Park, California: Lane Book Company, 1964.

Kroeber, Alfred Lewis, *Cultural and Natural Areas of Native North America*. Berkeley: University of California Press, 1939.

————, *Handbook of the Indians of California*. Washington, D.C.: Smithsonian Institution, Bureau of American Ethnology Bulletin 78, 1925.

Lummis, Charles Fletcher, *The Spanish Pioneers and the California Missions*. Chicago: A. C. McClurg & Company, 1929.

Odell, Ruth, *Helen Hunt Jackson*. New York: D. Appleton-Century Company, 1939.

Older, Mrs. Fremont (Cora Miranda), *California Missions and Their Romances*. New York: Coward-McCann, 1938.

Palou, Francisco, *The Founding of the First California Missions*. San Francisco: Nueva California Press, 1934.

Pitt, Leonard (editor), *California Controversies: Major Issues in the History of the State*. Glenview,

Mission San Miguel, famed for its cactus gardens and artifacts of the Spanish era, is now a parish church. (California Mission Trails Association Ltd.)

Illinois: Scott, Foresman and Company, 1968.

Pourade, Richard F., *The Explorers — The History of San Diego*. San Diego: The Union-Tribune Publishing Company, San Diego, 1960.

————, *Time of the Bells*. San Diego: The Union-Tribune Publishing Company, 1961.

Riesenberg, Felix, *The Golden Road, The Story of California's Mission Trail*. New York: McGraw-Hill Book Company, 1962.

Robinson, Alfred, *Life in California: A Historical Account of the Origin, Customs and Traditions of the Indians of Alta-California*. Oakland: Biobooks, 1947.

Sanchez, Nellie Van de Grift, *Spanish Arcadia*. Los Angeles: Powell Publishing Company, 1929.

Saunders, Charles Francis, *The California Padres and Their Missions*. New York: Houghton, Mifflin and Company, 1915.

————, *Capistrano Nights; Tales of a California Mission Town*. New York: R. M. McBride and Company, 1930.

Tibesar, Antonine (editor), *Writings of Junipero Serra*, 4 volumes. Washington, D.C.: Academy of American Franciscan History, 1955.

Vancouver, George, *A Voyage of Discovery to the North Pacific Ocean and Round the World, in the Years 1790, 1791, 1792, 1793 and 1794*, 3 volumes. London: G. G. and J. Robinson and J. Edwards, 1798.

A U. S. Army lieutenant made this sketch of San Diego in 1853 before it fell into ruins. (Security Pacific National Bank)

1

Prelude for the Mission Era

.

FOR NEARLY a century, the Spanish missions stretching from San Diego to north of San Francisco Bay along El Camino Real *(The Royal Highway)* formed the only centers of civilization and culture in California. They nourished the first pueblos, which gradually grew into cities after the impact of gold's discovery and the coming of the Americans.

High speed freeways have replaced the dusty El Camino Real, which during the late eighteenth and early nineteenth centuries at times hugged the coast and then turned from cliffs into the more easily travelled valleys, returning later to the seaside. Despite modern highways and urban growth, visitors can still enjoy the quiet charm of the Spanish missions. Each of the twenty-one establishments is distinguished by its individual architecture, marked by varying degrees of Spanish, Moorish, Mexican, and Indian traditions.

The picturesque "mission" architecture has inspired, with adaptations, themes for public buildings, office structures, residences, park edifices, hotels, and railroad stations. The mission or rancho tradition in turn has nurtured outdoor living and entertainment that is so closely identified with California.

Prelude for the Mission Era

California's history is a recent one in comparison to Europe's or even to the eastern United States. While America's eastern seaboard, Mexico, and South America were being colonized by the British, Spanish, French, and Portuguese during the sixteenth and seventeenth centuries, the area that was to become California was virtually neglected. In fact, the civilized world hardly knew that the place existed.

The first word of the area came to the Spanish, who being active on the Pacific Coast of South America logically attempted northward explorations. One such party sailed in 1534, just 42 years after Columbus discovered the New World. The expedition's commander was killed by mutineers. Their leader, Fortun Jimenez, found his way to what he believed was an island — but which really was Baja

Carmel Mission, with its beautiful lines, is restored and stands in a seaside setting.

Father Francisco Garces pioneered exploration of the desert approaches to California, urging establishment of missions. His statue stands at Bakersfield.

California. Indians killed Jimenez, but survivors returned with word of California to Hernando Cortes, the conquistador. He failed in an attempt to establish pearl fisheries at the tip of Baja California. The barren land offered few promises and the Spanish withdrew — virtually ignoring the region of California proper for more than two centuries.

California received its name at approximately this time. A contemporary form of "science fiction," *The Deeds of Esplandian*, was popular. It described, among other things, a place inhabited by Amazons called the "Island of California" — said to be near the "Terrestrial Paradise" and "at the right hand of the Indies." Since Cortes apparently expected to discover an island of the legendary Amazons in the area, his men — probably familiar with Montalvo's book — apparently bestowed the name "California" on the region.

Present-day California actually was discovered by Juan Rodriguez Cabrillo, a Portuguese navigator sailing for the Spanish crown in search of a shorter way to China. He reached San Diego Bay on September 28, 1542 — fifty years after Columbus discovered America. Cabrillo apparently explored the coast as far north as Monterey. He died of an injury in early 1543 and his crew explored the coast to possibly near the present Oregon-California border before returning with the reports. The Spanish crown, content with exploiting Mexico and South America, was not interested in California. During the ensuing years, ships of the Manila galleon — carrying merchandise from the Philippine Islands — skirted the California coast en route to Acapulco but seldom made landings.

California's next visitor was Sir Francis Drake, who explored the area in 1579 during his circumnavigation of the globe. He named the land Nova Albion ("New England") and claimed it for the British crown, an action that eventually would be a factor in establishing the Spanish missions.

Not until 1602 did the Spanish show increased interest in California. Sebastian Vizcaino, a Baja California pearl fisher, was authorized at that time to explore the area. Sailing up the coast of California, Vizcaino bestowed names that remained during the Spanish and American periods: San Diego, Santa Barbara, Carmel, and Monterey, among others. His enthusiasm equalled that of a modern Chamber of Commerce official and he sought permission to establish a settlement at Monterey. Spanish officialdom rejected the proposal, preferring to devote the energy and money to explorations which

This drawing of Mission San Buenaventura in 1829 appeared in Alfred Robinson's "Life in California" and showed the outpost thriving. (Security Pacific National Bank)

eventually proved worthless.

Meanwhile the Spanish extended the frontier of New Spain to northern Mexico, where missions were founded in the late sixteenth century. Barren and dry, California was written off as a worthless desert island — until proved otherwise by Father Eusebio Kino, an Italian-born Jesuit whose particular skill was making maps. Indians at Yuma in 1699 gave him shells similar to ones he had seen in Baja California. His subsequent explorations, in 1702, determined that California was part of the continent, and he argued successfully for establishing a mission chain on the Baja peninsula.

This chain grew, with the Jesuits in charge of the establishments. The Jesuit influence ended in 1767, however, when the Spanish crown expelled the order from all royal possessions because of the strong and controversial influence the body exer-

cised in Europe. The Franciscan Order was assigned the duty of directing the Baja California missions.

Coincidentally, other nations began to show an interest in present-day California.

The Russians, easily crossing Bering Strait, were active in the Alaska fur trade and were interested in moving southward. The British were pushing across Canada to the Pacific Coast. The Spanish, with logic, featured that Russia or Great Britain eventually would attempt to colonize California which was inhabited only by Indians.

At this point, the Spanish crown ordered the viceroy ("vice king") of New Spain to investigate Russian intentions. The directive was interpreted as a command to settle California. The decision to establish missions, therefore, was a political one based on the desire to secure California rather than one designed only to bring Christianity to the Indians.

Indian Tribal Areas

Religious holidays were occasions for spectacular ceremonies involving all attached to the mission. This early 19th century sketch was made of such an event at San Juan Bautista. (Security Pacific National Bank)

2

The Indians: Contrasts in Culture

·

THOSE WHO CAME first to California found it considerably different from today: while smog fortunately was lacking, neither were there palm trees or gardens to add beauty to the California landscape or elaborate aqueducts to bring water. The coastal plains and inland valleys where the missions would be built were arid and covered by shrubs, oak trees, and, in spring, fields of mustard grass and wildflowers. Rivers carried sizeable amounts of water only during infrequent rainstorms; the rivers then wandered here and there, changing courses according to the strength of the downpours.

California, then as now, was a land of contrasts. The rainfall averages from up to forty inches in the redwood forests of Eureka to approximately twenty inches at San Francisco, fourteen at Los Angeles and eleven at San Diego. Most of the rain comes from November to March, and summers are dry but mild. Fogs rolling in from the sea often creep miles inland. Dry and unirrigated, the countryside is typically brown or yellow, but becomes green for a few months after the winter rains. Mountains parallel the sea and rise abruptly above plains and valleys; during the winter, the tallest ranges are covered with snow. There are earthquakes — most of them mild, but periodic ones so strong as to leave severe damage.

The 800-mile coast — more than the distance from the southern tip of England to the top of Scotland — also is one of contrasts. Beaches stretch for miles, only to be interrupted by cliffs rising abruptly from the ocean. Early-day travelers often were forced to journey through the inland valleys to avoid the dangerous and virtually impassable shore line.

The Indians to whom the Spanish sought to bring their brand of civilization were considerably less picturesque than those of the American Plains and Eastern Seaboard or Mexico. There were, however, many of them: the pre-Spanish population of California is variously estimated at between 100,000 and 150,000 — or, in effect, one-eighth of all Indians in the present-day United States.

15

A Russian visitor sketched these Indians, typical of those native to the area, in 1816 at San Francisco. (Bancroft Library)

California Indians fashioned fish hooks from bones. (Southwest Museum)

This early sketch depicted a typical California tribal ritual of cremation, which included burning the deceased's belongings. (Bancroft Library)

Anthropologists credit this relatively large population to California's mild climate, which made survival easier than in areas with radical changes in the weather.

The Navajo, Zuni, Aztec, and Indian cultures represented comparatively advanced stages of civilization. These Indians established cities, cultivated crops, and lived under stringent laws. By contrast, the California Indians lived under more primitive or Stone Age conditions and were separated from other Indian cultures by the barriers of deserts and high mountains.

It is difficult to generalize descriptions of the Indians because of regional differences in California's terrain and climate. Anthropologist Alfred Louis Kroeber, a leading authority on the state's Indians, even warned against the correctness of applying the term "tribe" to them because of the great differences. The more accurate unit of division was the village, which the Spanish called *rancherias*. California had 1,000 to 2,000 small Indian villages, each containing fifty to two hundred people. The settlements were small to avoid overuse of the undeveloped resources.

The California Indians lacked the handsome features and impressive bearing identified with other American Indians, according to Kroeber. They were short and had small skulls with flat noses and broad faces. The Indians had no common language: anthropologists have identified at least twenty-two linguistic families and estimate that as many as 150 dialects were used. A barrier as simple as a river could separate dialect "areas" and people in nearby villages therefore would find it difficult or even impossible to converse.

The difficulty in communication, coupled with limited resources, resulted in little commercial trading or social exchanges between villages. Seldom did Indians travel far from the places where they were born. In fact, to venture far from one's village was dangerous: people in other *rancherias* might attack "invaders" who presumably sought their supply of food.

The Indians apparently were above average in intelligence. With arrival of the missionaries, they learned Spanish quickly and many even mastered Latin for worship services. They learned to read music and sing and also became skilled weavers, seamstresses, carpenters, tilemakers, farmers, and cattleherders.

Prior to arrival of the Spanish, Indian culture varied geographically. Where the climate was mild,

This hut, built of tree branches and mud, is typical of Indian homes in the pre-Spanish era. The Spaniards taught the Indians how to build with adobe.

many Indians took advantage of the weather by wearing little or no clothing. The extent of garments apparently was linked to the cold or warmth of various areas, and ranged from brief aprons to robes. In the warmer coastal areas, the men wore nothing and the women went topless but wore front-and-back aprons which would be "mini" even by modern standards. Depending on local availability and customs, these aprons were made from plant fibers or buckskin. Many Indians went barefoot, although when footwear was used those in the northern part of the state wore moccasins while those in the south more often used sandals.

Records indicate that until the arrival of the Spanish, the Indians did not suffer from diseases such as measles, smallpox, tuberculosis, influenza, or syphillis. They were apparently plagued, however, by lice, fleas, and vermin from animal skins in their houses.

The Indians' religions were primitive by modern standards, but held to a belief in immortality; eternity was a place of joy and plentifulness without work or problems. One widely held belief traced time back to a distant era when a raging sea covered the plains and all but the highest mountains. Virtually all humans were destroyed, according to this belief, except the few who climbed the mightiest

These Indians lived in a typical California adobe at Mission San Fernando. (Security Pacific National Bank)

peaks. Religious beliefs varied regionally, but many revolved around the animals with which the Indians were familiar.

Community organization was loose: while villages had a nominal chief, he exercised little real power. Many families created their own laws and discipline. There were no systematic regulations for conduct or punishment for misdeeds. Inter-village (or tribal) warfare was rare and when it did occur usually involved quarrels over acorn groves or fishing places.

The men who came carrying the flag of Spain and the Cross of the Catholic Church were to introduce these Indians to the basics of European civilization.

Housing also varied greatly according to area, with climate playing a great part in the type of construction. Indians in the northern section of the state, where there were many trees, built houses primarily of lumber. In central California, dwellings were half above and half below the ground, with wood slabs cut from trees forming the roofs and sides. The Chumash, who lived in the area from roughly San Luis Obispo to Ventura, constructed half-round houses of poles covered with grass or dirt.

The American pioneers contempously — and improperly — referred to the natives as "digger" Indians because roots provided part of their diet. Their most important food, however, were acorns from the oak trees which grew so abundantly on the coastal plains and valleys. The Indians mastered the task of hulling the acorns and then leaching the tannic

acid from them. They ground the acorns into meal with rock pestles and mortars. This meal, with fish and nuts, became an important part of the Indian diet. The Indians, using bows and arrows as well as lances tipped with flint, also hunted birds and animals. Rabbits, lizards, squirrels, coyotes, deer, quail, crows, snails, and snakes were among the things that rounded out meals. The Indians believed bears were possessed with demons and did not attempt to kill or eat this animal.

California Indians were distinguished for weaving fine baskets. (Southwest Museum)

The California Indians were not skilled in pottery-making, but they achieved excellence in basketry, a skill that basically occupied women. They used baskets for purposes ranging from utensils for cooking to containers for storage.

Many examples of intricate baskets and other products of the California Indians are displayed at the Southwest Museum in the Highland Park area of Los Angeles. The museum itself is devoted almost entirely to the preservation of material relating to the culture of the American Indian.

The Spanish used three instruments in their conquest of the New World: the *presidio* or fort, the *pueblo* or city, and the *mision* or church mission. While all three were used in California, the missions were the most effective instrument in this extension of civilization.

This 1847 sketch was one of the earliest illustrations made of San Luis Obispo, approximately halfway between Los Angeles and San Francisco. (California State Library)

3

The Founding of the Missions

THE CROWN designated the Franciscan order, which in 1767 had assumed control of the missions in Baja California, to establish the ones in Alta California. The order was founded by Saint Francis of Assisi (1182-1226), a native of Italy. He must be acknowledged, regardless of religious beliefs, as one of time's great personalities. His teachings — and his life — exemplified humility, love of poverty, devotion to other men, and religious fervor. *The Prayer of Saint Francis* helps express his teachings:

Lord, make me an instrument
of Your Peace

Where there is hatred, let me sow love
Where there is injury, pardon;
Where there is doubt, faith;
Where there is despair, hope;
Where there is darkness, light;
Where there is sadness, joy;

O Divine Master, grant that I may seek not so much to be consoled as to console; to be understood as to understand; to be loved as to love; for it is in giving that we receive; it is in pardoning that we are pardoned; and it is in dying that we are born to Eternal Life. Amen.

The Franciscan order was divided into three organizations: the Friars Minor Capuchin, the Friars Minor Conventional, and the Friars Minor (once called Observants and consequently given the "O.F.M." abbreviation often found at missions or in religious literature). Those who founded the California missions belonged to the latter group.

The Franciscans were trained to operate schools, but primarily served as missionaries. Members of the order earlier had missionary experience in Texas, New Mexico, and the Sierra Gorda of Mexico. The California experience was hardly a new one for the order. The Franciscans ingenious adaptation to the area and use of available skills and labor helped give the California missions their beautiful variations in architecture.

Father Junipero Serra, president of the California missions, became the personality most widely identified with the chain. In the years to come, the outposts popularly were called "Father Serra's Missions" despite the impact of other personalities of their ultimate success.

He was born in November 24, 1713, in Petra, a town of 2,000 people on the Spanish island of Ma-

Father Junipero Serra founded the mission chain. (Security Pacific National Bank)

jorca in the Mediterranean. On that same day he was christened Miguel Jose Serra in the parish church of San Pedro, on Calle Mayor just two blocks from his parents' home. His parents were farmers and devout Catholics. Dominating the plain of Petra was the hill of Bon Any, crowned by the chapel of the town's patron saint, Nuestra Senora de Bon Any (Our Lady of the Good Year), which then as now was a destination of devout pilgrims. A fellow missionary, Father Francisco Palou, wrote that "from his childhood, he was of a grave, benevolent, serious character, and his greatest pleasure was in attending the church. . . ."

Near his home was the convent church of San Bernardino, attached to a Franciscan monastery. The boy Serra mastered Latin, became skilled in chants, and sang in the church choir — each day fervently aspiring to become a Franciscan. He entered the order when sixteen years old. He then adopted a new first name: Junipero, after a companion of the order's founder. Serra was greatly impressed by Brother Junipero's tenderness and about whom Saint Francis once remarked, "Would that I had a forest of such trees."

Serra studied devoutly. Father Palou wrote later of Serra's training that "his zeal and exemplary conduct endeared him to his superior, and the brethren of the order, who vied with each other in forwarding his views and perfecting his theological studies."

Father Serra served as a priest for fifty-four years.

Arriving in the New World when thirty-six years old, Father Serra served in the missions of the Sierra Gorda in the Mexican state of Quesetaro prior to a 1758-1767 assignment at the College of San Fernando in Mexico City. He then was president for a year of the missions in Baja California.

Travelling in Mexico soon after his arrival, Serra was attacked by insects and left permanently lame. Yet during future travels he repeatedly refused treatment, being a believer in mortification or suffering of the flesh for purification of the spirit.

Even his fellow clerics placed Father Serra's devoutness far above the average priest. While recognized as an outstanding evangelist, he insisted on showing his faith with constant devotions. He carried asceticism to extremes by modern day standards, although in this respect he was similar to many priests of his era.

Founding the Missions

By 1768, fearing that Russia or Britain would establish outposts in California, the Spanish had formulated a plan for colonization by founding missions, forts, and pueblos to secure the land for the crown. Soldiers and missionaries, rather than settlers, formed the initial expedition. The plan was later to bring colonists, who with the native Indians would form cities. Three ships and two land expeditions started for California.

Heading the first land party was Captain Fernando de Rivera y Moncada, who commanded twenty-five "leather jacket" soldiers — named for their sleeveless jackets of tough leather designed to shield them from arrows — and forty Indians from Baja California who would build roads and help pacify the new area's natives. There were also three muleteers. Father Juan Crespi was chaplain.

The other land expedition was headed by Captain Gaspar de Portola, the project's military commander, and Father Serra. Their party included approximately ten soldiers and forty-four Indians from established missions.

One ship, the *San Jose*, perished on the way and no one aboard was heard from again. The other two ships reached San Diego in April, 1769. Blazing the trail over land, Captain Rivera's party arrived there on May 14. The second party reached San Diego on June 29; with it was Father Serra, riding a mule while recovering from an inflamed foot.

The era of California's Spanish missions was beginning.

20

The first step was establishment of the presidio ("fort") of San Diego, around which the original pueblo grew. This settlement later became "Old Town" when the modern city moved to its present site.

On July 16, 1769, Father Serra officiated for the founding of the first establishment which was destined to grow into a chain of California missions. The initial structure, hastily erected, was little more than a grass and mud hut — a far cry from the picturesque buildings that eventually would rise. Mission San Diego later was moved to its present site farther inland in Mission Valley.

families; some committed offenses against Indian women. Another difficulty was the lack of ample supplies of beads and other trinkets inasmuch as the expedition was backed by only minimum funds. Trinkets were deemed necessary tools in arousing the Indians' interest and showing friendliness to the newcomers.

A year passed before the first conversion at San Diego. The situation was typical of the early days at virtually every mission. Most of the first converts were children, women, and elderly people. The men joined later.

Father Serra was 56 years of age when he arrived

The "presidio" or fort was a Spanish institution used, along with the missions, to bring Hispanic culture. This is the presidio at San Francisco. (California Historical Society)

Many members of the expedition were ill on arriving at San Diego. While Father Serra and others in the party remained at San Diego to care for them, Portola went northward to locate Monterey — the point where the Spanish crown had directed the establishment of a port and settlement. The party seeking Monterey, incidentally, discovered San Francisco Bay, which previously had escaped explorers.

Building the Chain

Attracting the Indians to Christianity initially proved a difficult task. One problem was the attitude of the soldiers, all of whom were without wives and

in California. His age and illnesses made his establishment of the missions in a barren land even a greater accomplishment than would have been the feat for a younger and healthier person.

Some historians argue that Serra was more pugnacious than required in his advocacy of the missions' authority and rights. His defenders claim that he indeed must have been correct, noting that the records show the Spanish high authorities usually decided controversies in favor of the missionaries instead of the military or civil authorities.

Each state is represented by two of its distinguished personalities in the National Statuary Hall

Three ships left Baja California with supplies for the projected missions. The San Antonio *reached San Diego in a few days, but the* San Carlos *arrived there only after a 110-day trip. The third, the* San Jose, *was lost at sea with all aboard.*

in Washington, D.C. California's selections were Starr King, a Unitarian minister of the Civil War era, and Father Serra.

Father Serra's fame has travelled internationally.

The second mission established was San Carlos Borromeo de Carmelo, later popularly called "Carmel Mission." Father Serra officiated for its founding on June 3, 1770, at Monterey, where a presidio was established at the same time. The mission was moved a few miles away to a site at the present city of Carmel and opened there in December, 1771. Some historians say the move was made because the presence of soldiers hampered the conversion of Indians; Father Geiger, the noted Franciscan historian, says that his research indicates the real reason for moving to Carmel was to be nearer Indian villages and the proximity of fresh water.

The original mission building in Monterey became a chapel for those attached to the presidio. The Presidio Chapel, with a facade of stone and its other walls of adobe, has endured — with repairs and reenforcements — through the years and stands on Church Street in Monterey.

Despite the problems of obtaining converts and the limitation of funds, the Spanish were determined to establish more missions. The founding of San Gabriel and San Antonio de Padua came in 1771, while in the following year San Luis Obispo was established. In 1776 — the year in which the Liberty Bell was ringing out on the other side of the continent — the bells of San Juan Capistrano and San Francisco de Asis first chimed. Santa Clara de Asis was founded in 1777.

While the chain grew rapidly for such a barren area, the missions had not yet begun to prosper. The Indians, indignant over the religious and civil control sought by the Spanish, showed their ire by attacking some missions. Approximately 800 Indians attacked San Diego on November 4, 1775, killing one priest (Father Luis Jayme) and burning the mission buildings.

Life in California during the early mission period was something of an ordeal: obtaining basic necessities was difficult and the Spaniards had to be on guard for hostile Indians. Supply ships often were late and when coupled with occasional crop failures, the situation brought desperation. Hunting parties would comb mountain areas for bears and other game to fill the larder pending arrival of ships or the harvest of crops.

The colonization of California began in 1776 with the arrival of Captain Juan Bautista de Anza, probably one of the New World's ablest frontiersmen, with a party of settlers. Leaving Arizona with 240 people, he crossed the most desolate portion of the desert with only one loss of life (a woman died in child birth). He arrived with 241 people (two children, including the one whose mother died, were born along the way). The casualty rate among the gold seekers who came nearly a century later was tremendously high despite comparative modernization of equipment. They had no Juan Bautista de Anza to guide them.

The settlers formed the nucleus of California's first two cities: San Francisco (a site personally selected by Anza) and Los Angeles.

A New Leader for the Missions

Father Junipero Serra died August 28, 1784, at Mission Carmel, where he was interred. He was three months away from his seventy-first birthday and had been a Franciscan for fifty-four years.

Taking his place as president of the mission briefly was Father Francisco Palou, 61, who departed in 1785 for the College of San Fernando in Mexico City and two years later completed his biography of Father Serra. This work became a basic reference for historians dealing with Serra and the California missions.

Incidentally, the administration or chain of command over the missions was simple. Two padres directed each mission. They were responsible to the "father-president," with headquarters at Carmel. He in turn received orders from — or made requests to — the Franciscan Order's College of San Fernando in Mexico City.

The padres, being Spanish, brought a Spanish version of Catholicism and their goals included helping the Indians to adapt themselves to contemporary Hispanic culture. In this respect, their roles did not differ from modern Catholic or Protestant missionaries who bring their own nation's culture along with religious teachings.

Men were the only members of a religious order present. Nuns arrived at the California missions only after the facilities were revived during the American period. Some drawings of mission plans depict a *monjerio* or *convento*, but there were dormitories for un-

Mission San Luis Obispo today is the central structure in a mall-like park in the downtown area.

married women rather than rooms for nuns.

With Palou's departure, Father Fermin Lasuen became president of the California missions. He was 49 years of age in 1785 when he assumed the office. While Father Serra earned the credit of conquering difficulties in founding the missions, it was under Father Lasuen's administration that they evolved into prosperous institutions.

Born at Victoria in the Basque province of Alava, Lasuen served at the College of San Fernando after arrival in the New World. He then was assigned to the California missions and in 1773 became supernumerary (assistant pastor) of San Gabriel, which was growing into one of the most prosperous of the outposts. Father Lasuen found a new challenge in supervising and building the mission chain. He also proved to be among the most affable of Spaniards to the few visitors to California during the period.

The first foreigner to visit Spanish California was a Frenchman, Comte de la Perouse, who in 1786 spent ten days at Monterey and later wrote with high praise of the missions' president.

"Father Fermin de Lasuen, president of the missions of New California," wrote the Frenchman, "is one of the most worthy of esteem and respect of all

ABOVE LEFT: Father Fermin Lasuen succeeded Father Serra as president of the mission chain in 1785 and established more outposts. ABOVE: Massive arches give character to Mission San Luis Obispo. BELOW: Mission San Buenaventura (center) dominated Ventura's business district when this photo was made in 1874. (Security Pacific National Bank)

the men I have ever met. His sweetness of temper, his benevolence, and his love for the Indians are beyond expression."

The words contained more than polite praise, for Perouse was critical in his writings about other Spaniards.

George Vancouver, the British navigator, visited California in 1792, 1793, and 1794. Although a Protestant, he expressed great admiration for Lasuen.

"This personage," Vancouver wrote, "was about 72 years of age, whose gentle manners, united to a most venerable and placid countenance, indicated that tranquil state of mind that fitted him in an eminent degree for presiding over such a benevolent institution."

Vancouver erred in his appraisal of Father Lasuen's age and his statement was accepted as fact by historians for years. Father Geiger, the Franciscan historian, determined that Lasuen was born in 1736. This would have made him only 58 years old at the time of Vancouver's final visit.

So great was Vancouver's esteem for the president of the missions that in naming the two reaches of San Pedro Bay he honored the priest: Point Fermin and Point Lasuen remain on maps as the northern and southern points of the bay.

Under Father Serra, the missions were limited in their outreach and concentrated on farming and cattle-raising. By contrast, Father Lasuen "industralized" the missions. He encouraged the migration of artisans from Mexico, thus giving the Indians instructors in the fields of masonry and carpentry. The number of missions doubled and so did the number of converts.

The first mission established under Father Lasuen's presidency was Santa Barbara, founded in 1786. The other eight (and the dates of founding) started while he headed the chain included La Purisima Concepcion, 1787; San Juan Bautista, 1790; Soledad and Santa Cruz, 1791; San Miguel, San Fernando, and San Jose, 1797, and San Luis Rey, 1798.

Most interestingly, it was during Father Lasuen's presidency that the mission structures began to assume the architectural lines that distinguish them today. His presidency was a time of expansion: the original missions were small buildings, and as the outposts flourished these structures were demolished and replaced by more spectacular edifices.

Father Lasuen was an exceptionally active man. In 1797, when 61 years old, he not only presided over the founding of three missions but made visits — a most difficult task because of the era's primitive

La Purisima's bells hang in a campanario, a wall built as an extension of the mission with openings.

roads — to the other outposts in the chain. Lasuen proved himself an outstanding and dedicated leader, but history accorded him a relatively small place in history because he followed in the shadow of Father Serra.

Father Lasuen died at the age of 67 on June 26, 1803, at Mission Carmel. He was buried there.

Succeeding him was Father Estevan Tapis, who was president until 1812. Other presidents of the missions and their terms were Fathers Jose Senan, 1812-1815 and again in 1819-1823; Mariano Payeras, 1815-1819; Vicente Francisco Sarria, 1823-1825; Francisco Duran, 1825-1827; Jose Bernardo Sanchez, 1827-1831; Narciso Duran, 1831-1838 and again in 1844-1846, and Jose Joaquin Jimero, 1838-1844.

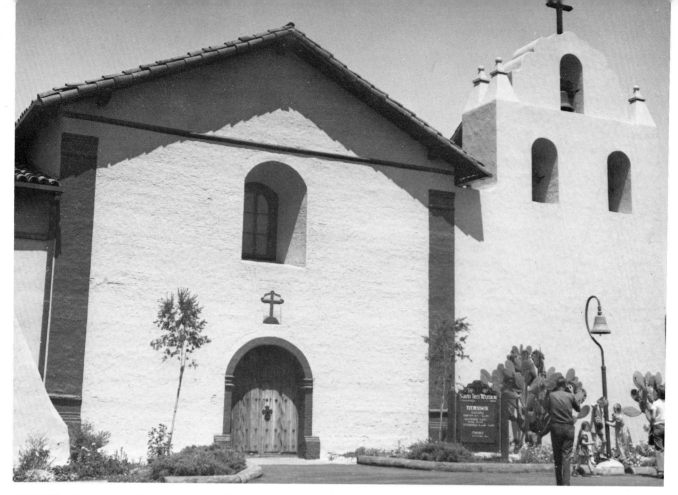

ABOVE: A spectacular cactus garden is a feature of Mission San Miguel. BELOW: San Miguel's cam- *panario, or wall holding bells, stands in front of the cemetery where Indians were buried.*

26

This 1846 sketch of Mission San Diego showed its lines before it fell into ruins. It was rebuilt with a companario, or bell "wall," instead of the bell tower shown here. (Security Pacific National Bank)

4

How They Built The Missions

THE FRANCISCANS who directed building the mission structures were trained in a variety of fields, as indicated, and previously had worked in other pioneering areas of New Spain. Since they lacked the finances to hire skilled artisans from Mexico who could design, engineer, cut stone, and provide woodworking refinements, they therefore made do with the materials and labor at hand. They began training the Indians, whose previous knowledge of building techniques was confined to crude dwellings, in construction skills.

The first mission structures were considerably different than the more substantial structures the Spanish built later: they were buildings of wood poles with tules or brush for walls and roofs.

As the missions prospered and grew, their distinctive architecture developed and the buildings dominated the countryside. The fact that the government sent artisans from Mexico starting during the Lasuen era made more skills available and resulted in the more substantial and attractive buildings. The missions certainly were the most noticeable and spectacular structures on the undeveloped plains and valleys.

Four basic materials went into the later mission buildings:

Adobe Bricks. Made from a mixture, in water, of chaff, straw, earth, and even manure, the adobes dried in the sun (as opposed to being baked in a kiln as bricks). Pieces of brick and shells sometimes were placed in the mixture to give cohesiveness. These adobes were approximately ten by twenty-three inches in dimensions, and two to five inches thick. Wet clay was used as mortar to hold the bricks together. The weakness of adobe limited the heighth of such walls to approximately thirty-five feet; then timbers were placed in the wall to give strength. Trees large enough to provide adequate timber in many cases were a considerable distance from the mission sites. Indians used oxen to haul timber for miles. The higher the structure, the thicker were the adobe brick walls: some were up to six feet in width

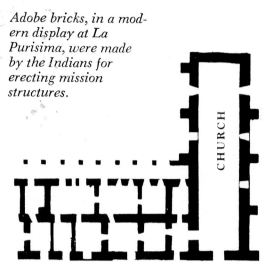

Adobe bricks, in a modern display at La Purisima, were made by the Indians for erecting mission structures.

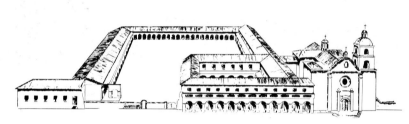

ABOVE: This floor plan of Santa Ines shows the narrow chapel, typical of missions because of limited materials and skills. LEFT: The drawing of San Luis Rey shows the usual mission plan — a chapel stood at a corner of a quadrangle formed by buildings containing workshops and quarters. (Both Drawings: California Mission Trails Association Ltd.) BELOW: Mission San Antonio de Padua after reconstruction.

Pioneer artist H. O. Ford reflected Mission Santa Barbara's majestic architecture in this drawing made during the early 1800's. (Security Pacific National Bank)

and two feet in thickness was not uncommon. The disadvantage to adobe brick was that unless protected, they melted in the rain. Most adobe walls therefore were whitewashed or plastered inside and out.

The floor plans of the missions, which included many structures in addition to the sanctuary, followed a similar pattern throughout the chain. The purposes were to provide areas for worship, work, and living quarters. The sanctuaries — the principal section of the missions that today's visitors see — usually were placed at the northeast corner of the quadrangle forming the mission compound. The other three sides provided dormitories for the Indian girls and unmarried women, housing for the priests, barracks for soldiers, a kitchen where food was cooked for all attached to the mission, and shops. The latter included facilities for weavers, tanners, shoemakers, carpenters, and blacksmiths. These buildings formed patios where trees and gardens were cultivated.

As previously indicated, these walls were up to six feet thick due to unskilled labor. The rare excep-

tions were the cases where skilled stone masons were available. Here are other characteristics which distinguished the missions architecturally:

Timber. Most of the missions were in valley or plain areas relatively near the coast where there were few trees of substantial size. The Indians cut trees in the mountains paralleling the coast and hauled the timber to the mission sites. This was often a considerable task; for example, Indians hauled timber 40 miles to the place where Mission San Miguel was being erected. The lumber was used to reinforce the walls or to form doorways or window openings. The narrowness of the mission chapels resulted from the fact that only relatively light timber was readily available. This forced reduction of the sanctuaries' width so that there would be adequate support for the tiles or mud covering the roofs. The church sanctuaries, therefore, typically were long and narrow. For example, the widest inside dimensions of any of the mission churches were twenty-nine feet at San Carlos, Santa Cruz, and Santa Clara; the inside widths were only 18.3 feet and 16.2 feet at Soledad and San Francisco So-

ABOVE: *This portion of an aqueduct at La Purisima is typical of those built by Indians at the missions. BELOW: The companario with bells at Santa Ines, pictured from the cemetery at the rear.*

lano respectively. What could not be accomplished in width was compensated for in length: Santa Barbara was 162.5 feet long even though only 27.5 feet wide, and San Fernando was 153.9 feet long but only 25 feet wide.

Facilities for milling timber was limited. The workmen used axes and crude saws to shape lumber and in some cases utilized poles or logs after only stripping the bark. These techniques added to the beauty and distinctiveness of the mission structures.

Stone. Artisans skilled as stone masons were not available at most missions, at least during the early period. The inexperienced builders therefore used a softer sandstone, which was relatively easy to cut but which did not resist the elements as well as would have stone selected by artisans. Lacking lime mortar to provide the best bond for the stone, the priests and Indians followed the Mexican pre-Columbian technique of using mud mortar, into which was mixed colored stones and pebbles. The result was a beautiful and interesting texture.

In a few cases, experienced stone masons were available. For example, San Juan Capistrano was constructed almost entirely of stone under the direction of Isidro Aguilar, a mason from Mexico.

Brick and Tile. Assuring much greater endurance, *ladrillos* (conventional bricks) were fired in kilns and varied in size according to their intended use. The square ones for floors ranged from eleven to fifteen inches across. Those used as common brick typically were approximately ten inches square and three inches thick. They were extremely durable: columns made of such brick at La Purisima Concepcion stood for years after the adobe walls crumbled.

Tejas (roof tiles) were used in later construction to replace the flamable straw roofs. They were made by molding the clay mixture over a section of a log, and usually were twenty to twenty-four inches long. They tapered from ten to five inches in width. Father Geiger, the Franciscan historian, reports his research shatters two myths widely used in books and history classes regarding the mission tiles. Legend has it that the tiles first were used at Mission San Luis Obispo while in fact, he notes, Mission San Antonio de Padua really was the first to use such roofing. He also reports that there is no evidence the tiles were molded around the legs of Indians and that the logs actually were used to achieve their semi-roundness.

Belfries. Mission architecture provides four basic ways to hold church bells. The primitive or basic belfry consisted of a bell hanging from a beam sup-

30

ABOVE: This cross stands against a weathered wall at Mission San Jose.

BELOW: This deeply recessed window at La Purisima illustrates the thick walls that were typical of mission architecture.

ABOVE: This view of the side of Mission San Buenaventura's sanctuary shows examples of the heavy buttresses designed to support walls. BELOW: A detached bell support helps distinguish San Rafael.

This rear view of San Antonio shows how the campanario provided a facade for the mission.

stated earlier, were uniformly long and narrow. The size of the timber available for supporting the roofs restricted the width of the santuaries. The builders compensated for the narrowness — and created another distinctive facet of mission architecture — by constructing relatively long chapels.

Supporting Buttresses. The fact that the priests and Indians lacked advanced engineering skills and building materials forced them to resort to thick walls in an effort to achieve permanency and protection against earthquakes. In addition, the sides of many sanctuaries were braced on the outside with massive buttresses which were typically thick at the bottom and smaller at the top. Experts also have suggested that since since these buttresses provided only minimum safeguards against earthquakes, their usage may have perpetuated the traditional lines of the fortress churches of Mexico and the architecture of medieval Spain.

Arches and Corridors. The long corridors formed of arches also distinguished the fronts of most missions, serving practical as well as esthetic purposes. They provided protection from rains in the winter and from heat during the summer. The arches were Roman or half-round. The design of the pillars varied at individual missions, but usually were square. Most were constructed of brick, making them more durable than the adobe buildings they fronted. The graceful arcades typical of mission architecture can be viewed at San Fernando, San Luis Rey, Santa Barbara, San Miguel, San Diego, La Purisima, Santa Ines, San Luis Obispo, and San Juan Bautista, among others.

Decorations. Lacking trained natives or the funds to hire sculptors from Mexico, the missions relied on the Indians executing carvings from stone and wood with designs apparently copied from books. Simple but artistically effective designs were carved on the keystones of stone arches, on facades, over doorways, and even on doors.

Native artists often painted the interior walls of sanctuaries with religious paintings. Those remaining or restored show the flavor of the Spanish era, mixed with the primitive touch of the Indian artists.

Although Father Geiger's research shows the glass was ordered from Mexico for Mission San Luis Rey, the mission structures themselves usually were devoid of glass in the windows. The latter were recessed considerably because of the thick walls. Simple chairs, tables, and benches — usually unpainted — furnished the rooms. Light came from tallow candles made at the missions.

ported by two posts; an example has been reconstructed at San Francisco de Solano at Sonoma. A second method is the campanario, consisting of a wall — with openings for bells — attached to the sanctuary building or even standing alone. Examples of the attached wall are at Santa Ines and San Gabriel, while the campanario at San Antonio de Pala illustrates the detached type. The third variation is the Espadaña, which is a raised gable — usually curved and decorated — at the end of a church building; San Diego provides an example. The last type is the well-known tower, which can be seen in various forms at San Luis Rey, Carmel, San Buenaventura, and Santa Barbara.

The Naves. The main sections of the churches, as

*Open fields and the background of mountains help,
even today, to give Mission Santa Ines the feeling
of early California's pastoral era.*

5

Life in Pastoral California

·

THE MISSIONS gradually attracted Indians. Some came initially because of curiosity or gifts offered by the padres and remained because of the attraction of religion or the better life seemingly offered at the missions. Others followed when relatives or friends told them of the protected and benevolent — even though regimented — life they enjoyed in the system.

The padres did not force conversion, which was a voluntary decision for each Indian. Once the decision to embrace Catholicism was made, however, the Spanish regarded the choice as irrevocable. Work and worship at the missions then was required.

Some Indians spurned the missions: the outposts could claim only approximately 30,000 converts out of the estimated 100,000 to 150,000 natives in California. More possibly would have decided to be converted except for their lack of contact with the missionaries because of distances.

When converted, the Indians were known as "neophytes" (newcomers to a religion). They lived in villages usually standing approximately one hundred yards from the mission buildings. The crude mud or straw huts of pre-Spanish times were replaced with more substantial dwellings. These were often houses of adobe with roofs of brush or in some cases (Santa Barbara or San Gabriel, for instance) with tiles. A typical day began at sunrise, with the mission bells calling the Indians, soldiers, and others attached to the mission to mass. Following a worship service came a breakfast of *atole*, a broth made of roasted barley cooked without seasoning.

The Indians then went to their various duties in the fields, shops, sewing rooms, or caring for cattle. Most missions had many cattle, and proudly used their own brands on the livestock. The cattle were reared not only for food but also for their hides and tallow, which were traded to the ships that called. Many missions had orchards of olive trees; the olives were ground, on crude presses, for olive oil also traded to ships that carried the produce primarily to Mexico or the United States. Most labor around the

A popular game with the mission Indians was throwing sticks upward and betting on whether an odd or even number would fall. This sketch was made in 1816 by an artist who visited California with a Russian expedition. (Bancroft Library)

missions was performed by hand: the era lacked an abundance of sophisticated machinery, and lack of funds and the distance from Mexico made it difficult to obtain equipment. Some historians have contended that the fathers were not enthusiastic in acquiring time-saving machinery because they felt Indians with time on their hands would fall into evil ways. Catholic mission historians strongly deny such statements, claiming that the padres were quick to use any labor-saving device available and pointing to the greatful acceptance of skilled help offered by Joseph Chapman and other settlers or California visitors.

The labor duties assigned to the Indians probably was no greater — and possibly lighter in some respects — than those endured by farmers in America during the same period of primitive agricultural methods. Sherburne F. Cook, in his *The Conflict Between the California Indian and White Civilization* which is critical of the mission system, at one point concludes that much of the work "would be classed today as light labor. It is very significant that even the bitterest opponents of the missions never accused the clergy of giving the Indians work which might cause either excessive fatigue through extremely long hours or physical injury through intense exertion and occupational hazard."

Shortly before noon the Indians left their tasks for a meal of *pozole*, a thick soup of vegtables and muttom or beef. They returned to work in the afternoon to work for approximately an hour and an half, except during the sowing or harvest season when the hours were extended.

The Indian work-week therefore averaged out to thirty to forty hours spread over five or six days, according to the season. This schedule was one that American union members battled to attain in the late nineteenth and early twentieth centuries.

During the afternoon the Indians rested, played games, visited, or pursued studies in religious dogma.

The evening meal again was *atole*.

The Indians were not necessarily confined to this diet. Many raised chickens and went hunting or fishing to supplement the mission or "community"

This early sketch shows riders from a mission capturing a grizzly bear. (California State Library)

menu with home cooking. Fiestas and other special occasions, of course, brought barbeques and the serving of tastier foods.

Sundown again brought the mission bells calling everyone to a period of worship.

At night, women whose husbands were away and those who were not married were secured in the mission *convento* under the careful eyes of matrons — who were trusted Indian women or the wives or soldiers — and not permitted to emerge until daylight. This precaution deterred pre-marital or extramarital sex activity.

Indians believed in living in harmony with nature. As mobile food gatherers, they constantly moved from place to place. Aware that the Indians were itinerant and not conditioned to set working schedules, the missionaries tried to assign reasonable tasks. There were many Indians, of course, who could not be conditioned to a Spanish mold and who thus rebelled.

Mission life, of course, brought a revolution in wearing apparel for the Indians. The Spanish initi-ally brought cloth from Mexico and later raised sheep which provided wool for fabrics. The Indians' nude or semi-nude state gave way to apparel befitting the Hispanic culture that was developing.

There were times for recreation and games as well as prayer and work. Alfred Robinson, an American trader who visited Santa Barbara in 1829, described a competition in which 200 to 300 Indians competed with a wooden ball in a game involving "presidio" and "mission" teams. They also had foot races and games in which Indians alternately guessed in which hand another concealed a stick.

Among the most spectacular and gory of amusements, also described by Robinson, were the bear and bull fights which the Indians staged, usually in front of the mission. The procedure was for the Indians to trap a bear in a nearby hill area, lasso him, and bring the animal to the mission. The next day the bear and a bull battled in a fenced area while the Indians cheered. The match usually ended with the death of the bear.

The missions lacked schools in the modern sense of

ABOVE: Missions were self-sufficient, particularly during their early years. This wheel at La Purisima ground meal.

BELOW: Cooking was a communal affair at the missions. This massive outdoor oven can still be seen at San Miguel.

the meaning. The Indians learned the skills of agriculture, animal husbandry, building, shoemaking, weaving, and sewing as they worked. Converts and children learned the beliefs of Catholicism during daily services; at the same time they learned the Spanish language.

The missions' remoteness from other centers of civilization precluded the availability of hospital and medical care by present standards. The priests, whose training managed to cover many areas, diagnosed illnesses and gave treatment.

The limited "self" government permitted consisted of the Indians annually electing an *alcalde*, who usually was a person approved by the padres at the involved mission. The *alcalde*, assisted by two *regidores* who performed duties similar to justices of the peace, made sure that the Indians of the pueblo observed the routine prescribed by the Spaniards.

There were relatively few violent uprisings against the Spanish; when wars erupted, they usually were inspired by older Indians who resented the regimentation of mission life. The mission system accomplished the goal of bringing civilization to a pre-agriculture people. Amazingly, a handful of Spaniards — 45 priests at the peak of the mission period and 300 soldiers — were able to control more than 30,000 Indians with little bloodshed in comparison to that which flowed in the American West.

The mission system was a paternalistic one, presided over by padres who sought to be benevolent. The Indians who made the decision to be converts to Christianity found themselves in a regulated society providing a mixture, in varying parts, of security, order, work, worship, and regulation. The padres apparently regarded their roles as ones to provide spiritual guidance but also to train the Indians so that some day they could live independently as craftsmen, artisans, farmers, and ranchers. The priests, it should be emphasized, regarded their mission system as a temporary custodian of vast acreages which would be given eventually to the Indians.

As benevolent and idyllic as the system appeared, one wonders in retrospect if California's isolation prevented the padres from realizing that rapidly changing times and circumstances — unrest in the Spanish empire and the American movement to the West — would not frustrate and destroy the mission system.

In regard to the Indians, most who became converts considered the mission system a great improvement over their previous primitive way of living. Many *rancherias* (Indian villages) disappeared as

ABOVE: This beehive-shaped oven at La Purisima was heated by charcoal and baked bread. BELOW: San Carlos Cathedral, still standing in Monterey, was used by Spanish soldiers.

37

The Cuartel, *or jail, was a part of the mission where offenders were punished. This facility is at La Purisima.*

their residents abandoned them for life at the missions. The Indians both loved and feared the padres, and apparently believed that the priests miraculously were in direct contact with God.

Not all Indians liked mission life. Those of the second generation adapted best to the system, for it was the mission instead of the *rancheria* that nurtured them. Many adult men, usually ones from Indian villages, refused to adhere to mission discipline and routine. Some escaped successfully and joined bands that stole mission cattle and crops.

While Indians who became converts were expected to remain under mission domination, the Spanish did not force them to remain throughout the year at the establishments. The Indians received frequent "vacations" of one or two weeks to visit their native villages. They also were given "days off," on request, for fishing or other recreation. The harvest season was the busiest for the missions, and the In-

dians were expected to work more diligently at this important time.

Spanish California's system of justice provided various forms of punishment for violations of the era's standards of morality or order. Mission fathers maintained that Indians never were punished without an explanation of the reason. Missions had no formal jails. First offenders received an oral reprimand. Repetition brought corporal punishment ordered by the padre and carried out by soldiers. This punishment, in order of its severity, consisted of the stocks, shackles, and the lash.

Offenders spent one to three days in the stocks, according to the seriousness of the situation, and this was the most commonly used form of punishment and usually the only one inflicted on women. Indians who insisted on trangressing were placed in shackles while continuing to work. The lash was reserved for those who repeatedly violated the rules.

Andrew P. Hill's painting of Mission Santa Clara in 1849 caught the spirit of vitality that pervaded the outposts before their decline.

6

The Golden Age of the Missions

THE MISSION chain prospered the greatest during the late eighteenth and early nineteenth centuries. Individual missions thrived in varying degrees according to the fertility of the lands and local conditions, trading with merchant ships from the United States and Mexico. It should be understood that a mission comprised much more than the buildings; lands of an individual mission could stretch for miles, since there were virtually no private holdings. Soledad, a smaller mission, boasted 20,000 acres, while missions such as San Antonio and San Miguel each had more than 200,000 acres. The land surrounding the mission buildings was used for orchards, vineyards, farming according to soil and climate conditions, and grazing.

The missions and a few privately-owned ranchos were the most prominent landmarks and stopping places for the few travelers who made their way along El Camino Real with business in the principal secular settlements: San Diego, Los Angeles, Santa Barbara, Monterey, and San Francisco. This was the era that popularly was called the "Golden Age" of the missions.

Folklore and misinformation picture the brown-robed padres welcoming travelers and the townspeople staging fiestas at the drop of a sombrero. The mission fathers most certainly earned a lasting reputation as genial hosts, but the color of their robes was gray. Not until 1885 — well after the end of the Spanish mission period — did the Franciscans begin wearing the brown robes. Fiestas were given at the end of cattle round-ups and for some religious occasions, but these parties were far from weekly affairs. For the relatively large private landowners, life was pleasant and easy. But for the average citizen who worked on a ranch or at a trade, survival required much effort in that era before the forty-hour week and minimum wage laws.

The Golden Age found little friction between the missions and the handful of settlers then in California. Many Indians attached themselves to the missions, which offered a better life than that which

ABOVE: A fortress-like front distinguished Mission San Gabriel Arcangel, surrounded by lush farmlands and vineyards in this nineteenth century sketch. (Security Pacific National Bank)

BELOW: Missions administered vast last holdings during the Spanish period, but lost their power during the Mexican era. This map shows the holdings of Mission San Rafael in 1834.

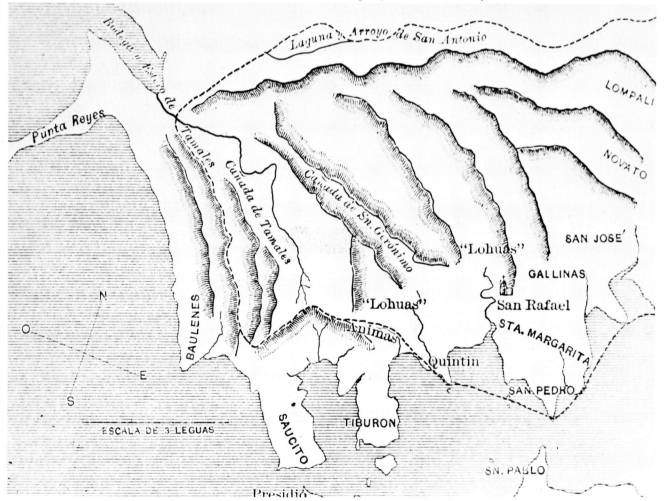

they were accustomed.

The mission chain itself was nearing completion. Santa Ines, nineteenth in order of founding, was established in 1804 with Father Estevan Tapis officiating. The site of the Santa Ines River north of Santa Barbara was selected because of the dense Indian population and a fear that the villages' proximity to more warlike tribes in the interior would result in troubles. The final two missions established were San Rafael and San Francisco Solano, both north of San Francisco Bay. San Rafael was founded in 1817 to relocate Indians in a milder climate after illness and death plagued San Francisco. While intended to be a sub-mission or *asistencia* of San Francisco, San Rafael after 1823 appeared as a mission in official reports. San Francisco Solano was established in 1823 at present-day Sonoma to serve as a northern safeguard against the Russian fur trappers then active in nearby coastal regions.

Among the most prosperous missions was San Luis Rey; in 1815 one of its ministers, Father Antonio Peyri, established an inland branch to serve the immense Indian population. The *asistencia* was named San Antonio de Pala and became noted for its detached campanile. Pala never became a full-fledged mission, but it is distinguished today as the only post in the chain still primarily serving Indians.

Incidentally, travellers were greeted cordially at the missions and received food and lodging — both given graciously without charge. Sojourners found little for amusement, however, since the pueblos hardly compared to the booming cities of Mexico or Spain and the missions themselves were places for work and worship. If the guest was among the few of the era who could read, he would enjoy browsing through the mission libraries. Despite California's remoteness, many of the libraries contained books covering a wide range of subjects: history, medicine, fiction (*Don Quixote*, for example), biographies, and architecture. The libraries, of course, also had many volumes relating to sermons and the lives of saints.

During the 1700s and early 1800s, the missions — along with a handful of ranchos established on a few land grants made by the Spanish crown — were virtually the only outposts of civilizations. The missions, each approximately a day's ride by horseback apart, were convenient and genial places for travelers to stop for the night.

The California countryside at this time was open and there were few fences. The few existing roads

This early sketch showed a typical vaquero *or cowboy who worked with mission herds. (California State Library)*

were hardly more than dusty trails. Except for occasional fogs near the ocean, the days were bright and clear. Visibility in this era before factories, freeways, autos, and tract homes was so good that virtually every day one could see details of canyons in the mountains while miles away at the seashore.

The era was relatively free of violent crimes and in retrospect appears as a leisurely, almost lazy time when the greatest pressures were those of the routines of periodic worship and a few hours of work in a field or orchard.

TOP: *Father Narcisco Duran,
sketched with an Indian child,
was president of the mission
chain from 1831 to 1838. CENTER:*
Vaqueros *round up cattle at a
rancho. BOTTOM: With independence from Spain, Mexico
granted more ranchos, and cattle
roamed the California countryside.
These* vaqueros *join in a roundup.
(California State Library)*

This sketch shows La Soledad in 1883, when buildings were crumbling following collapse of the mission system. (Security Pacific National Bank)

7

The Decline of the Mission System

.

T HE GOLDEN DAYS of the missions began to close in the 1820s. News of Mexico's successful revolution against Spain, won with strong anti-Church overtones, reached California in 1822. The era brought an atmosphere of distrust of the padres and others of Spanish birth. The new Mexican government's program included secularization of the missions, or in effect taking control of the vast acreages held in trust by the Catholic Church for the Indians and placing this land under civil or government administration.

Seculurization in reality reduced the missions to parish churches, devoid of the surrounding acreages administered by the priests and worked by the Indians.

Most historians agree that the secularization of the missions was a complicated matter and one that is difficult to explain in a few words. The first step in the California program of secularization was Governor Jose Echeandia's 1826 decree permitting Indians to leave the missions if they had been attached to them for a substantial number of years. A few did so, but their training had not prepared them for the trials of living in a world of sophistication and greed. The government initially approached the secularization program cautiously, recognizing the control and guidance exercised by the padres over the Indians.

Meanwhile, the Mexican government made extensive land grants — contrary to the Spanish policy of keeping such assignments of land at a minimum and maintaining extensive church control. This more generous land policy, of course, encouraged the Spanish and Mexican settlers to seek control of the acreage held for the Indians by the missions.

Governor Echeandia in early 1831 initiated a program for secularization by converting the missions into civil pueblos and giving each Indian family an allocation of land and livestock. The padres would remain at the missions as pastors.

The program brought chaos to the Indians and the properous missions. Many Indians gambled away

Another sketch of La Soledad, made after secularization, shows the sanctuary still standing even though surrounding buildings were decaying. (California State Library)

their property, refused to work at the missions, and were reduced to lives of begging or stealing.

Changes in the central Mexican government brought a new governor for California, Manuel Victoria, who slowed — but could not stop — the closing of the missions. Revolutionaries ousted Victoria and after counter-revolutions the Mexican government in 1833 appointed Jose Figueroa to the office of governor. While some historians name Figueroa as the man who destroyed the missions, he apparently had mixed feelings regarding their importance in California.

The central Mexican government's policy was that the paternalistic mission system was not compatible with the nation's democratic goals. Figueroa toured the missions observing their operations and

hearing the padres' protests over secularization. He concluded that the missions were not ready for civil control and that it would be best for the Indians to remain under the padres' "parental" jurisdiction at least temporarily. The governor's recommendation came too late, and a Mexican government decree in August, 1833, called for secularization of the missions. The decree unfortunately permitted vast acreages belonging to the missions — as trustees for the Indians — to fall into the ownership of individuals.

Undaunted by the decree, Governor Figueroa sought to make secularization a gradual process. He converted only a few missions at a time into parish churches by dividing half the land and livestock among the Indians and placing the remainder under control of secular administrators.

Figueroa's good intentions were frustrated by his death in September, 1835, after which unscrupulous adminstrators enriched themselves and friends through misuse of mission property. Lack of care caused buildings to decay, cattle to be killed needlessly, and farmlands to lie idle. So badly did the missions fare that one of the first acts of pro-clerical Manuel Micheltorena on being appointed governor on Dec. 31, 1842, was to return the missions to administration by the padres. The hope for renewed prosperity for the missions was short-lived, however, because of pressures from the improvised central Mexican government and Micheltorena's ultimately

eral neglect as parishioners moved elsewhere caused most of the mission buildings to fall first into disrepair and then into ruins.

By 1847, when the United States achieved supremacy over California, the mission lands were in the hands of private owners and many mission buildings were in ruins.

The Indians themselves fell from a world in which they were highly protected into one where they were used and abused. This, along with disease, poverty, and the arrival of Americans who further victimized them during the 1850s gold rush, help to decimate them. There are relatively few descend-

The quadrangle of buildings at San Buenaventura was beginning to decay in this 1870 photo. Vats and presses for olives and grapes are in the foreground.

being forced from office after a power battle among the growing number of California settlers.

The new governor, Pio Pico, was anti-clerical and presided over the demise of the mission system.

The mission lands were given as grants to settlers and animals were stolen under the eyes of civil authorities while the Indians watched — helpless and confused as the system to which they had grown accustomed collapsed. With surrounding land falling into private hands and the Indians leaving, the mission establishments began to decline. Some priests left for assignments in Mexico, while a few remained at the missions — attempting to maintain the structures and serve a rapidly diminishing number of parishioners.

The task proved too great for a handful of priests and church-goers. Floods, rains, vandals, and gen-

ants of the mission Indians remaining in California. The bulk of California's Latin American population traces its ancestry to people who came from Mexico beginning in the early twentieth century.

The American period brought involved disputes over Spanish and Mexican land grants that were eventually resolved in the United States Supreme Court. The Catholic Church was awarded the mission structures, cemeteries, orchards, and surrounding gardens.

Even though the missions declined, they formed the nucleus for many cities. The Spanish wisely selected sites according to the availability of water, access to good ports, and the proximity to other natural resources essential for thriving communities. Major cities began to grow where missions once were the only evidence of civilization.

LEFT: Although decaying in the late 1800s, missions began to attract those interested in Spanish California culture. These visitors inspected the ruins of La Soledad. (California Historical Society)

BELOW: An 1886 photograph showed people on an outing who stopped to explore the ruins of Mission San Fernando Rey. Formations of adobe brick remained, although some had melted into mud. (Security Pacific National Bank)

Santa Ines originally had nineteen arches, forming a pleasing arcade identified with the missions. Ten arches survived when this photo was made in the 1970s.

8

The Preservation of the Missions

THE MISSION structures themselves might have disappeared into mounds of mud had not numerous individuals — many of them Protestants — become interested in the buildings, their heritage, and the handful of Indians they were serving in the late nineteenth century. Here is the cast of characters and the roles each played:

Helen Maria Hunt Jackson (1830-88). A native of Maine, Mrs. Jackson's primary work was writing children's stories until the late 1870s when, during a visit to California, she became interested in the plight of the Indians. She subsequently served on a United States commission considering their problems. Her 1881 book, *A Century of Dishonor*, criticized American policies to Indians. Her novel, *Ramona*, was published in 1882 in an effort to bring popular attention to the Indians' ordeal; the highly romanticized book became one of the most popular volumes of the day.

Abbot Kinney (1850-1920). A tobacco company magnate and later developer of the Santa Monica Bay communities of Ocean Park and Venice, Kinney became concerned over the treatment of Indians and served with Mrs. Jackson on the federal commission that studied ways to protect them. His interest in the Indians extended to preserving the missions.

John Stephen McGroarty (1860-1944). A Democratic member of the U. S. House of Representatives, McGroarty used his skill with the pen to fascinate the public and remind them of the Spanish heritage: *The Mission Play* was housed in the Mission Playhouse, erected near Mission San Gabriel. During the play's seasonal presentation, extra schedules of the Pacific Electric's Big Red Car trolleys carried thousands to see the drama revolving around the missions.

George Wharton James (1858-1923). Using his literary skill, James dramatized the missions' history in books and gained public support for their preservation and restoration. His books included *Old Missions and Mission Indians of California* (1895) and *In and Out of the Missions of California* (1905). He

Charles F. Lummis, an editor and student of Indian culture, took a leading role in preserving the missions.

John Stephen McGroarty's The Mission Play *developed interest in Spanish California culture. (Both Photos: Security Pacific National Bank)*

also lectured extensively on the missions.

Father Zephryn Englehardt (1851-1934). Born in Germany and brought to America as an infant, Father Englehardt served as a Franciscan missionary among Indians for more than twenty years before becoming the order's full-time historian in 1903. Using materials from mission archives and other sources, he wrote prolifically and in detail regarding the Spanish era of California. His publications spurred the interest in missions with professional and lay historians.

Charles Fletcher Lummis (1859-1934) A native of Massachusetts and son of a Methodist minister, Lummis was a man of many interests and probably took the greatest role in preserving the missions and Indian culture. He arrived in Los Angeles in 1885 after a 3,507-mile "sightseeing" walk in 143 days from Cincinnati. En route he sent articles about the trip to the *Los Angeles Times* and on arrival was greeted by the publisher, Harrison Gray Otis, at Mission San Gabriel.

Lummis was, at various times, the newspaper's city editor, head Los Angeles librarian, and the

leader in founding the Southwest Museum in Los Angeles, which preserves Indian culture. He rounded out his career by residing five years with the Indians at Isleta, New Mexico, to learn their culture. Despite these activities, he built a fifteen room house — at the rate of one room a year — on Avenue 43 in Los Angeles; standing by the Pasadena Freeway, it is now a state historic monument open to the public.

Among Lummis' major accomplishments was founding of the Landmarks Club in 1895 for the purpose of preserving the missions and other historic buildings. For his success in preserving Spanish architecture, he was knighted by the king of Spain.

Once the decaying mission buildings were saved from further ruin, historic and civic organizations, as well as the Catholic Church, began reconstructing them so that the structures would again appear as during their "golden" days. Early drawings or photographs were studied carefully, as were descriptions written during the mission days.

Some restorations were excellent: buildings at San Antonio de Padua and San Luis Rey, for example, were carefully rebuilt along their original lines. Some restorations lacked authenticity: a mission "style" structure was built at Santa Cruz on the site of the original edifice because few details were available, and San Francisco Solano at Sonoma was reconstructed as a museum without following architectural lines shown in early photographs.

"De-Americanization" was required in some restorations. Lumber placed over the adobe walls at San Luis Obispo was removed as part of restoration. A New England-style steeple required remodelling at San Juan Bautista to restore the Spanish lines. Santa Barbara, one of the most beautiful of the missions, was used continuously by the Franciscans and retained its lines through the years.

Archaeological excavations and restorations are continuing today at several missions.

Note: Information on dates and the scope of restoration is included with the section on individual missions.

The crusade for preservation and restoration pressed by Mrs. Jackson, Mr. Lummis, and their contemporaries accomplished its goal of stirring public interest in the missions. For instance, virtually every visitor to southern California during the twentieth century's first three decades took the Old Mission Trolley Trip, which carried sightseers on the Pacific Electric's Big Red Cars to San Gabriel — stopping directly in front of the mission. Commercialism, too, managed to profit from the picturesque image of the missions. The All-Year Club of Southern California (later appropriately renamed the Southern California Visitors Council) used the missions in advertising designed to draw out-of-state tourists. The California Mission Trails Association (later given the name California Mission Area Association to broaden its appeal) issued publicity aimed at encouraging motorists to vacation along El Camino Real. Both organizations drew support from motels, restaurants, gas stations, real estate developers, and others who expected to profit from the travelers.

Novels, picture post cards, souvenir maps, and motion pictures revolved around the California missions. Among the greatest salutes to the Spanish heritage was the Mission Inn at Riverside: the massive hotel's architecture incorporated domes, arches, corridors, towers, and other distinctive features from the original missions. Thousands of visitors paid for guided tours and many people selected the hotel's Spanish-style chapel for weddings. Richard Nixon and Patricia Ryan were married there in 1940.

Helen Hunt Jackson's novel, Ramona, *called attention to the plight of the Indians and helped preserve the missions. (Security Pacific National Bank)*

49

Spanish mission architecture has made an impact on California building design. This mission-style structure is at Hunter Liggett Military Reservation and stands a few yards from Mission San Antonio de Padua.

9

The Mission System in Retrospect

·

PHILOSOPHERS of varied convictions today debate the good and negative points of the Spanish mission system, just as they differ over the merits of other institutions and events of the past. Defenders of the mission system depict the era as an idyllic one of harmony during which dedicated padres helped the Indians move from a virtual stone-age culture of savagery into a civilized society enabling them to have better lives. Critics condemn the system with charges of extreme paternalism and authoritariansm giving the Indians little freedom and minimal training for assimilation into white society.

California Controversies is a fascinating book that deals with different sides of points of disagreements in the state's history. In the volume, Sherman F. Cooke—a University of California (Berkeley) physiologist — criticizes the mission system, and the respected Franciscan historian, Father Maynard Geiger, defends it. Dr. Cooke maintains that "there

can be no serious denial that the mission system, in its economics, was built on forced labor" and criticizes the Spanish for changing Indian cultural life. Father Geiger, in the rebuttal, denies that Indian life was so difficult and notes that the natives made frequent unsupervised excursions to their villages. "The fact that most of them returned to the missions," Father Geiger states, "appears to be conclusive evidence that life at the missions for the majority, at least, was satisfactory."

Much of the criticism of the mission system came during the earlier twentieth century when a subliminal "Catholic vs. non-Catholic" atmosphere pervaded many circles. In this period of ecumenical movements and better understanding of different religions, we can deduce that a fair judgment of the mission way of life probably lies somewhere between the past praises and condemnations.

History indeed shows that in California the Span-

◊ *Twin towers and a magnificent stone facade enhance the beauty of Mission Santa Barbara.*

51

Some Spanish architecture was "Americanized." Here is the way the Los Angeles Plaza parish church looked during the Spanish era.

By the late 1800's the structure had been remodeled with more traditional American lines. (Both Illustrations: California State Library)

ish endeavored to protect and civilize the Indians — in contrast to the policy in the American West of pushing them from land sought by settlers.

While communities have developed around most of the missions, each in its individual way continues to perpetuate the flavor of the Spanish era. The missions are open to the public: some offer individually-guided tours while others provide self-guiding literature. Nominal admission charges or donations usually are requested for these tours. These small fees

help to maintain the landmarks.

Every mission has its distinctive architecture and restful gardens. Many have rooms and even formal museums filled with picturesque artifacts which help visitors in visualizing the atmosphere of the era when the missions were California's only points of civilization.

There is no doubt that the missions will be attractions for travelers for many years to come, just as they have been for two centuries.

Edward Vischer, whose early California etchings are renowned, sketched this 1842 view of Mission San Gabriel. Note the open fields. (Security Pacific National Bank)

The Missions

from South to North

Made in approximately 1890, this photo showed buildings at Mission San Diego neglected and decaying. (Security Pacific National Bank)

San Diego de Alcala

CALIFORNIA'S first Spanish mission, both in order of founding and en route north along El Camino Real, is Mission San Diego de Alcala. The mission is at 11005 Friars Road in San Diego's Mission Valley. Visitors can reach it from U.S. Highway 80 by taking the Murphy Canyon turn-off.

The Spanish reached California in the early summer of 1769 to begin the area's settlement. After a brief rest to permit the travelers to recover from the difficult journey, Father Junipero Serra on the feast day of Our Lady of Mount Carmel — July 16, 1769 — called on the physically able to help erect a brush shelter.

This was California's first church.

Contrary to popular belief, San Diego is not translated "Saint James." The mission honors Saint Didacus, who was born about 1400 in Alcala de Henares, a town approximately 20 miles northeast of Madrid. Didacus, entering the Franciscan order, served as guardian of the group's community on the Canary Island of Fortaventura from 1445 to 1449, when he was sent to Rome. There he was credited with miraculous cures which won him sainthood.

The mission originally was situated at Presidio Hill and was moved to its present site in 1774. The outpost burnt in 1775 during an uprising of 800 Indians and rebuilding started the following year. By 1783 the mission began to assume something of its present day appearance.

By 1800 the mission's properties covered 50,000 acres and it owned 20,000 sheep, 10,000 cattle, and 1,250 horses.

Secularization, bringing loss of the vast acreage, was followed by rapid decline of the buildings. In 1931, the mission was painstakingly restored to the way it looked during its golden era and annually attracts thousands of visitors.

Distinguishing the mission are its impressive facade and its bell tower, topped with a cross.

Reconstructed, Mission San Diego now is a parish church and is open to visitors. The mission includes a museum. (Title Insurance and Trust Company)

ABOVE: Mission San Diego was in
ruins and reflected little of its past
glory when this picture was made
in the late 1800s. (California
Historical Society)

RIGHT: Indians built this dam on
the river above the mission. The
photograph was made in 1930.
(Security Pacific National Bank)

The detached companario architecturally distinguishes La Asistencia of Pala, built as a sub-mission of San Luis Rey.

NOTE: San Luis Rey thrived so that in 1815 Father Peyri established La Asistencia (or sub-mission) of Pala, noted for its companario detached from the main buildings. The station, directed by the Verona Fathers-Sons of the Sacred Heart Order, continues to serve an Indian population at the community of Pala and, like San Luis Rey, is open to the public.

San Luis Rey

ARCHITECTURALLY among the most distinctive of the missions, San Luis Rey de Francia is in a rural valley setting on State Route 76 three miles inland from Oceanside. Founded July 13, 1798, with Father Fermin Lasuen — successor to Father Serra as president of the chain — officiating, the mission was the 18th in order of establishment.

The mission honors King Louis IX, who ruled France 1226-70 and under whose reign Gothic architecture flowered with the building of cathedrals. Louis, who helped found the Sorbonne, died of the plague in 1270 while leading a crusade against Tunis. His personality was manly yet ascetic and pious; he won respect in the Moslem world as well as among Christians. Louis IX was canonized in 1297.

San Luis Rey, founded after the earlier missions began to thrive, prospered almost from the start. The foundations for the present structure were laid in 1815 and built according to the plans of the pastor, Father Peyri, whose ideas also contributed to the design of Mission Santa Barbara.

The mission lands were secularized under Mexican rule, but the buildings and immediately surrounding property were restored to the Catholic Church during the American period. The document signed by President Abraham Lincoln restoring the buildings shortly before his death is preserved in the mission museum. The mission was dedicated as a Franciscan college in 1893.

San Luis Rey is architecturally distinctive because of its emphasis of Moorish lines more than any other mission in the chain.

RIGHT: Moorish architectural lines are more dominant in San Luis Rey than any other mission in the California chain. (Photo by the Author)

BELOW: Even though decaying when this picture was made in the late 1800s, San Luis Rey retained its distinctive lines. (California Historical Society)

The picturesque fountain and bells at San Juan Capistrano attract thousands of visitors annually.

San Juan Capistrano

THE BELLS heralding the founding of Mission San Juan Capistrano rang out in 1776—the same year that the Liberty Bell in Philadelphia sounded the news of America's Declaration of Independence.

Since then, the beauties of Capistrano's gardens and buildings have been praised in songs, paintings, photographic studies, and literature.

The patron saint of the mission is John of Capistrano (1385-1456)), a fighting Italian priest who became a hero defending Vienna against the Turks.

The first attempt to establish the mission was made October 30, 1775, by Father Lasuen (later president of the mission chain)', but was abandoned because of the Indian uprising at San Diego. The mission was formally founded on November 1, 1776.

An earthquake on December 8, 1812, destroyed the mission chapel (completed just six years before) and killed 40 Indians who were worshipping. Few attempts were made to rebuild because of the political pressures against the missions.

San Juan Capistrano has been noted for the swallows which make their traditional return (from an unknown wintering place) on approximately March 19, St. Joseph's Day. Father Geiger, the historian, notes, however, that no early mission documents mention the "miracle" of the swallows' return nor does he recall references to the event as a boy in Los Angeles early in the 20th century. He speculates

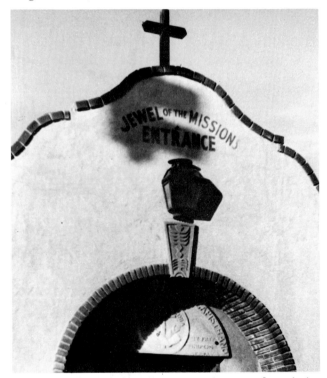

"Jewel of the Missions," a term given to the mission by its aficionados, is inscribed on the entrance to San Juan Capistrano.

that the legend developed during the early 1930s as a result of a widely read newspaper columnist devoting space to the birds.

In recent years, fewer swallows have been noted and ornithologists say the birds may be forsaking the mission because the surrounding area is becoming densely populated.

Whether the swallows continue to spend spring and summers at Capistrano or not, the mission and its gardens will remain colorful attractions.

Features of the mission include Serra's Chapel, believed to have been erected in 1777 (and given its name because the chain's president celebrated mass in the structure). The narrowness of the chapel is typical of early mission construction resulting from the limited timber available. Mission San Juan Capistrano is reached via turn-offs on U. S. Highway 101 in the city of San Juan Capistrano.

ABOVE: Artist Edward Vischer made this sketch of San Juan Capistrano when it was decaying in the mid-1800s. The massive ruin at the right is the church destroyed by the 1812 earthquake.

BELOW: A mission father at San Juan Capistrano chats with descendants of Indians who lived in the area and help erect the buildings. (Both Illustrations: Security Pacific National Bank)

Mission San Gabriel, with its harmonious architectural lines, has changed little since these visitors stopped in the late 1880s. (Security Pacific National Bank)

 # San Gabriel

MISSION SAN GABRIEL ARCANGEL, third in order of founding and fourth northward from San Diego, was established September 8, 1771, by Padres Angel Somera and Pedro Benito Gambon, who had been directed to build a mission 40 leagues north of San Diego.

Originally built in what is now Montebello, flood waters of the Rio Hondo caused its movement to the present site in San Gabriel in 1776. A permanent structure erected in 1796 was destroyed in the earthquake of December 8, 1812. Father Jose Maria Zalvidea supervised construction of the present mission building immediately thereafter.

While the less durable adobe formed the main construction material for most missions, stone, brick, and cement went into the sanctuary of San Gabriel. Other parts of the mission were built of adobe.

The mission's architectural lines are among the most harmonious in the chain. An outside stairway leads to the choir loft and belfry. The arches in the bell tower were designed to correspond to the different sizes of its bells.

In that by-gone era when the countryside was open grazing land devoid of subdivisions, autos, freeways, or factories, the bells of San Gabriel could be heard in Los Angeles — eleven miles away.

While most missions declined with secularization (or seizure of its land), San Gabriel survived since it was on the strategic overland route between Mexico and Monterey and near Los Angeles.

The mission's name honors Gabriel, the angel of good news.

The mission grounds contain ruins of soap vats, blacksmith shops, and kitchen facilities. There are also remnants of the mission's olive, pear and orange orchards, which were protected from wild animals by an extensive cactus hedge (parts of which can be seen in several parts of San Gabriel).

It was at Mission San Gabriel that the immigrants from Mexico gathered in 1781 to make the trip a few miles westward where they founded El Pueblo de Nuestra Senora la Reina de Los Angeles de Porciuncula, which began the spectacular growth that was to make it one of the world's great cities.

Mission San Gabriel is at 537 West Mission Drive, San Gabriel.

RIGHT: While less durable adobe was used for many missions, stone and brick went into the fortress-like walls of San Gabriel; note (at right) the outside stairway leading to the choir loft.

BELOW: The Mission Playhouse, near San Gabriel, follows Spanish architectural lines. It is the community's civic auditorium.

San Fernando Rey

THE 17th in order of founding among the 21 missions, San Fernando Rey de Espana was established September 8, 1797, by Father Fermin Lasuen, then president of the chain. The site was chosen because the area was the population center of the Shoshone Indians and was near several springs offering an adequate water supply.

The patron saint of the mission is King Ferdinand III (1198-1252), who united the Spanish kingdoms of Castile and Leon, and spent much of his reign in successful crusades against the Moors, re-establishing Catholic worship. He was canonized by Pope Clement X in 1671 and is the patron saint of engineers.

The mission's land was sold for $14,000 in 1846 to raise funds to defend California against the Americans. Later abandoned, the mission fell into ruins as looters removed rafters, tiles, and furnishings.

The Mexican sale was held illegal by the United States Supreme Court and the mission buildings, along with the immediately surrounding land, was returned to the Catholic Church in 1862. Reconstruction of the mission began in 1895 and the facility now appears basically as it did during its prime.

Mission San Fernando Rey's architecture has been used as a background for numerous motion pictures localed in Mexico or early California because of its proximity to the studios.

The distinguishing architectural feature of San Fernando Rey is the convent building, with its 21 beautiful arches facing the street. Other features include an Indian craft room with basket-weaving, part of the original mission kitchen, and a wine cellar near which is a small masonry footpath where Indians washed before trampling the grapes.

After the 1971 earthquake ruined the adobe church, plans immediately started to replace it with a sturdier structure.

Mission San Fernando Rey de Espana is at 15151 San Fernando Mission Boulevard, San Fernando — approximately midway between the Golden State and San Diego Freeways. Off-ramps noting the mission are marked on both freeways.

Palm trees framed the majestic arches of San Fernando Rey in this photo taken in the 1890s — long before housing tracts engulfed the Valley.

ABOVE: *Mission San Fernando Rey was decaying when this picture was made in 1904 by pioneer photographer C. C. Pierce, but civic groups worked for restoration. (Security Pacific National Bank) BELOW: The mission today, viewed from adjoining Brand Park.*

Mission aficionados John and Victoria Crump stand by a statue of Father Serra with an Indian boy in Brand Park. (Photo by the Author)

San Buenaventura

THE NINTH and last mission founded by Father Junipero Serra was San Buenaventura, established on March 31, 1782 — an Easter Sunday. The city of Ventura grew around the mission.

The mission's name honors Saint Bonaventure (1221-1174), a cardinal and doctor of the Catholic Church whose original name was Giovanni Fidanza. He was a member of the Franciscan order and was the author of the official life of Saint Francis.

A cross was erected during the early days (but not by Father Serra as some legends state) behind the mission on *La Loma de la Cruz* (The Hill of the Cross). This cross was downed by time and the elements, and a duplicate was erected in 1912.

San Buenaventura called early day worshippers with wooden bells — provided because of the shortage of metal. These bells now are in the mission's museum.

The mission suffered after secularization and was without a resident priest from 1840 to 1850, although a padre came from Santa Barbara for occasional services.

"Restoration" of the mission in the 20th century brought changes out of pace with its Spanish heritage. However, in 1957 — the 175th anniversary of the mission — the facility was remodeled in keeping with its appearance before its decline.

The address of Mission San Buenaventura is 211 East Main Street, Ventura.

BELOW: This 1875 picture shows Mission San Buenaventura; the cemetery adjoins the sanctuary. (Security Pacific National Bank) RIGHT: A modern view of the mission.

Santa Barbara

SANTA BARBARA is known as the "Queen of the Missions" because of its impressive architecture marked by Greek and Roman traditions. It is the only mission in the chain with twin towers.

The mission, tenth established and seventh in line from San Diego, was founded December 4, 1786, and formally dedicated twelve days later. Its patron is Saint Barbara, a third century martyr.

The earthquake of December 8, 1812, damaged a church building completed in 1794. The present church, dedicated in 1820, is among the sturdiest of all the missions. The sandstone walls are six feet thick in many places. Despite the care in building, the structure suffered severe damage in the 1925 earthquake. Pains were taken in repairing the church to restore the beautiful details of the original building.

Santa Barbara is the only mission where the Franciscan order has served continuously. Many early day documents, artifacts, paintings, statues, and other reminders of early California life are preserved in the mission's museum and archive-library.

The mission commands a panoramic hillside view of Santa Barbara and the surrounding coast. Its address is Upper Laguna Street, Santa Barbara.

This 1873 painting depicted the growing city of Santa Barbara. The mission is in the upper right area of the community; forming a backdrop is the Santa Ynez Mountain range. (Security Pacific National Bank)

ABOVE: Santa Barbara's massive stone facade and twin towers blend to make it among the most beautiful of the missions. (Southern California Visitors Council)

RIGHT: This photo of the mission in the 1800s was made when public interest in the chain was developing. (California Historical Society)

67

Santa Ines

S ANTA INES, 19th in the mission chain, was founded September 17, 1804, by Father Estevan Tapis, successor to Father Lasuen as president of the California missions. The site is on a knoll in the Santa Ynez Valley, a point from which the padres hoped to reach Indians in the Coast Range previously isolated from the outreach of missions.

The simple chapel first erected was damaged by the earthquake of December 21, 1812, and was re-placed by the present structure, completed in 1817.

The mission never attracted the large number of converts expected. Harsh treatment by soldiers resulted in the Indian uprising of 1824 which spread to Mission La Purisima and ended only after the arrival of soldiers from Monterey.

The patron of the mission is Saint Agnes, a child who died as a Christian martyr in the fourth century.

Santa Ines fell into ruins after secularization and its restoration was started in 1904 under direction of the late Father Alexander Buckler, who served as pastor until his retirement in 1924. Members of the Capuchin Franciscans of the Irish Province were placed in charge of the mission and have directed additional restorations.

Santa Ines' museum contains many exhibits pertaining to the early mission days.

The address of Santa Ines is 1760 Mission Drive, Solvang.

Mission Santa Ines stands in a rural area typical of California during the Spanish era.

ABOVE: This drawing by Edward Vischer depicted Santa Ines during the mid-1800s. (Security Pacific National Bank)

RIGHT: Note the details of the entrance to Santa Ines.

The Spaniards endeavored to improve the missions. This viaduct carried water to Mission La Purisima.

La Purisma

L A CONCEPCION Purisima de Maria Santisima (The Immaculate Conception of the Most Holy Mary) was founded December 8, 1787, by Father Lasuen, then president of the chain, as the 11th mission and eventually the ninth from San Diego in the completed group. The mission soon flourished and attracted a large number of converts.

The 1812 earthquake, which came on the mission's 25th anniversary, destroyed the mission and most of the surrounding Indian homes. The facility was relocated on its present site, which is approximately four miles northeast of the original area.

The Indians, directed by the energetic Padre Mariano Payeras, built the mission quickly, erecting adobe walls nearly four feet thick as protection against future earthquakes. Its lovely colonnade of 18 fluted columns supporting a low-sweeping tile roof was unique among the missions.

La Purisima, as the mission's name was abbreviated during the years, became the ecclesiastical headquarters for California in 1815, when Father Payeras was named president of the mission chain.

After secularization in 1834, the mission soon fell into ruins.

The property was acquired in 1935 by the state of California and reconstruction of the mission facility started with work being performed by the Civilian Conservation Corps, a federal agency for jobs during the depression.

Today, as La Purisima State Historic Park (on State Route 1 near Lompoc), the restored buildings represent a nearly complete mission. The project was designed to emphasize the economic side of mission life by depicting work areas and showing how the people of the era lived.

ABOVE: Square pillars, in contrast to round ones at some missions, formed the arcade at Mission La Purisima. (Security Pacific National Bank)

BELOW: Here is the companario at La Purisima, once in ruins but rebuilt with careful attention to details. The mission is now a state park.

San Luis Obispo

SAN LUIS OBISPO de Tolosa was founded September 1, 1772, by Father Junipero Serra as the fifth in the mission chain. It was an important link because at the time it was the only settlement between San Gabriel in the south and San Antonio de Padua, just below Monterey.

The patron saint is Louis, thirteenth century bishop of Toulouse and son of the king of Naples and Siciliy as well as the nephew of King Louis. for whom Mission San Luis Rey was named. Legend has it that California's first tiles were manufactured at San Luis Obispo as protection against hostile Indians firing burning arrows into the grass roofs. In fact, Father Geiger's research shows, the first tiles were made at Mission San Antonio de Padua.

The mission is now the center of a beautifully landscaped plaza in downtown San Luis Obispo, which grew around the mission and became an important stopping place since it was midway between Los Angeles and San Francisco. The mission's address is 782 Monterey Street and it serves as a parish church.

A printing firm occupied part of San Luis Obispo in the 1880s when its architecture was partially Americanized. (California State Historical Society)

ABOVE: Rolling hills, covered with oaks and brown grass during much of the year, were typical of the countryside surrounding the missions in central California.

RIGHT: The facade of Mission San Luis Obispo as it appeared in the 1970's.

ABOVE: Here is the gate that opens to San Miguel's gardens and cemetery. BELOW: The front of San Miguel's sanctuary, weathered with time, illustrates the functional design of the missions.

San Miguel

SAN MIGUEL ARCANGEL, alongside U.S. Highway 101 seven miles north of Paso Robles, is a particularly interesting mission to visit because its interior is so well preserved in its original condition. The decorations by Indians in many of the missions were damaged during restoration of the buildings.

San Miguel, honoring Michael, the angel who protects the good, was founded July 25, 1797, by Father Lasuen, then president of the chain, alongside the Salinas River, from which canals were built to irrigate the mission's crops. The establishment was 16th in order of founding and the 11th from San Diego when the chain was completed.

Fire virtually destroyed the mission buildings in 1806, resulting in the construction of the present structure, which was finished in 1816. Difficult times befell the mission after secularization in 1836. The last Franciscan at the mission died in 1841, and although the U.S. government returned the facility to the Catholic Church in 1859, there was no resident priest until 1878.

Today San Miguel again is under jurisdiction of the Franciscans and serves as a parish church.

The interior contains many decorations executed by Indians under supervision of the fathers and untouched since 1821. While the art work is crude, it reflects devotion and love. Of particular interest is the pulpit, which was decorated by Indians, and the huge rafters, hewn from trees brought 40 miles from the mountains. Among the mission's other art works is the "all seeing eye," representing an eye of God looking down on the earth.

The mission is surrounded by an attractive garden composed of many varieties of cactus plants.

San Miguel's famous cactus garden grows by the arcade attached to the sanctuary.

This photo of San Miguel in the 1850s shows that the mission's lines changed little with re-building. (Security Pacific National Bank)

San Miguel's sanctuary, photographed in the early 1900s, illustrates the narrowness dictated by lack of building materials. (Security Pacific National Bank)

San Antonio

THE THIRD mission founded by Father Junipero Serra was San Antonio de Padua, established July 14, 1771, in a beautiful valley by the Santa Lucia Mountains. Construction of the present church five miles west of Jolon (south of King City and north of Bradley) started in 1810 approximately a mile from the original site.

San Antonio de Padua was one of the largest as well as most beautiful missions. Its patron saint is Anthony of Padua (1195-1231), a Portuguese born Franciscan noted for his eloquence and who is popularly invoked by Roman Catholics for assistance in finding lost articles.

The mission stands in a valley where the San Antonio River flows to meet the Salinas River. The ample water supply helped wheat to flourish. The mission also gained fame for its fine horses.

Secularization brought neglect and ruin to the buildings, and not until 1903 were efforts made to save the outpost. At that time the Natives Sons of the Golden West began a campaign that resulted in partial restoration of the mission church. The quadrangle adjacent to the church was restored in 1950 with funds from the Franciscan Fathers and the Hearst Foundation.

The brick facade that adds distinction to the mission and the rural setting make San Antonio de Padua well worth a visit even though it is comparatively remote from highways. To reach the mission, one drives through the mountainous and wooden terrain of Hunter Leggett Military reservation. The mission is supervised by the Franciscan order.

The facade of San Antonio de Pala has delicate architectural details which distinguish it from other missions.

ABOVE: Although crumbling, the beauty of San Antonio de Pala still could be seen when this photo was made in the 1870s.

RIGHT: This picture of ruins of the aqueduct at San Antonio was made in 1923 before rebuilding of the mission. (Both Photographs: California Historical Society)

Soledad

ATHER FERMIN LASUEN founded Nuestra Senora Dolorosima de la Soledad (Our Most Sorrowful Lady of Solitude) on October 9, 1791, on a plain west of the Salinas River. The mission attracted converts slowly in comparison to the other outposts but it prospered until 1825, when political pressures caused its decline.

Although secularization forced the mission into poverty, its pastor, Father Vincente Francisco Sarria, remained with the Indians.

The church building started in 1808 was severely damaged by flood waters during the 1860s. With neglect, the mission was reduced virtually to piles of adobe mud by the mid-20th century. Reconstruction was started and a chapel built under auspices of the Native Daughters of the Golden West was dedicated in 1955.

The mission site lies in a rural area three miles southwest of the modern city of Soledad.

Soledad, as the mission is popularly called, was the 14th in order of founding and the 13th north of San Diego.

ABOVE: These mounds of adobe ruins remained at Mission Soledad in the 1970s while reconstruction of buildings was under way nearby. BELOW: These new mission structures stand on a portion of Soledad's original site.

ABOVE: This photo of Soledad in the 1880s showed the extent of the mission; rains eroded the adobe walls during the years.

BELOW: Edward Vischer's sketch showed Soledad in the 1850s before its decline. (Both Illustrations: Security Pacific National Bank)

Carmel

THE SECOND MISSION established by Father Serra was San Carlos Borromeo del Carmelo, one of the most beautiful in the chain. The mission was founded June 3, 1770, in Monterey and was moved to its present site a year later to take the Indians away from the influence of the military. The first mission became the chapel for the presidio.

The patron of the mission was Charles Borromeo (1538-84), a native of Italy and nephew of Pope Pius IV. Despite a substantial private fortune, he lived simply. He became a cardinal, administrator of the Papal States, and largely responsible for reopening of the Council of Trent. The Carmel Valley took its name from the Carmellite priests accompanying Sebastian Vizcaino on his voyage of exploration.

The mission, in a picturesque seaside setting, is noted for its gardens.

San Carlos Borromeo, sometimes called "Carmel" Mission, is on Rio Road in the southern part of Carmel-by-the-Sea.

ABOVE: Weathered walls and Spanish art await visitors at Carmel Mission. (Photo by the Author) RIGHT: This photo was made before restoration began in 1884.

Carmel was partially restored when this photo was made, probably in the early 1900's. Adobe ruins remained at the left. (Security Pacific National Bank)

San Juan Bautista

MISSION San Juan Bautista, honoring St. John the Baptist, was founded June 24, 1797, with Father Fermin Lasuen, president of the mission chain, officiating. The station was the 12th in the chain and the 15th north of San Diego.

The cornerstone of the present building was laid in 1803 and the massive structure — approximately 190 feet long — was completed in 1812. On retiring in 1812 as president of the chain, Father Estevan Tapis resided at the mission until his death 13 years later.

After being secularized in 1835, San Juan Bautista began to fall into ruins but was restored starting in 1884. A spectacular row of twenty arches distinguishes and adds beauty to the mission, which serves as the parish church for the community of San Juan Bautista. The mission, part of San Juan Bautista State Historic Park, is in a picturesque setting facing a plaza around which are an early day hotel, livery stable, and other buildings preserved to show a California town during the pioneer days.

ABOVE: This arcade at San Juan Bautista is typical of those at virtually every mission in the California chain. BELOW: A view from an arcade reveals the early California buildings which are part of San Juan Bautista State Park. (Photos by the Author)

ABOVE: An auto stopped by San Juan Bautista during an outing in the early 1900s when public interest was growing over the missions. Note the "Americanization" and use of wood in the tower. (California Historical Society) RIGHT: Here is the mission's sanctuary as it appears now.

Santa Cruz

THE 13th mission founded was La Exaltacion de la Santa Cruz. (The Exaltation of the Holy Cross), established September 25, 1791, on a site near what is now High and Emmet Streets.

The church building, completed in 1794, was relatively large — 112 feet long, 29 feet wide, and 25 feet high, with walls five feet thick.

An 1840 earthquake weakened the structure and an 1857 tremor destroyed the mission.

A replica of the mission, similar except that it is approximately one-half the size of the original, was constructed in 1931 on Emmet Street facing the Upper Plaza. This structure contains many objects removed from the original mission.

ABOVE: This parish church was constructed in 1931 on the site of the original Mission Santa Cruz and generally follows its architectural lines.

BELOW: This sketch of Santa Cruz was made in 1883 before the mission decayed. (Security Pacific National Bank)

ABOVE: Spanish mission architecture long has been an inspiration to artists. This group devotes its talents to the Santa Cruz reproduction.

BELOW: This sketch shows Mission Santa Cruz near its peak. An earthquake destroyed the buildings in 1857. (California Historical Society)

Santa Clara

MISSION Santa Clara de Asis is surrounded by the University of Santa Clara, Santa Clara Street and El Camino Real in Santa Clara. The school began as a college in 1851 and attained university status in 1912 after growing around the mission.

The mission was founded January 12, 1777, with Father Tomas de la Pena from Mission San Francisco de Asis officiating. The outpost was moved twice: in 1780 to avoid the flooding Guadalupe River and in 1818 because of damage caused to buildings by earthquakes that year and in 1812.

The third site (near the former ones) is where the present mission and university stand. Santa Clara's lands were confiscated in 1836 and the buildings began to fall into ruins. Rebuilding started in 1851 when members of the Society of Jesus, who still direct the facility, founded the college.

The adobe church started in 1822 and completed three years later was destroyed by fire in 1926. The present church, a replica of the original, was built in 1928. The patron of the mission is St. Claire, founder of the Franciscan order for women.

An attractive flower garden surrounds the mission, making an interesting foreground for photographs.

Santa Clara was the eighth mission founded and became the 17th northward from San Diego when the chain of 21 was completed.

This photo of Mission Santa Clara was made during the 1800s and reflects "Americanized" repairs. The University of Santa Clara was beginning to develop around the facility. (California Historical Society)

ABOVE: The highly respected University of Santa Clara, founded in 1851, grew around the mission. (University of Santa Clara)

RIGHT: A shaded walk by the mission provides a place for reflection and meditation. (Photo by the Author)

This photo of Mission San Jose apparently was made prior to the 1868 earthquake that destroyed many buildings. A wooden structure was then built for worshipers. (Security Pacific National Bank)

San Jose

THE 15th in order of founding, Mission San Jose was established on June 9, 1797, with Father Lasuen, president of the missions, officiating. It became the 18th northward from San Diego in the completed chain.

Among the reasons for establishing the mission was to gain a foothold along the eastern shores of San Francisco Bay. This area had been explored only slightly despite the Spaniards' nearly 30 years of activity in California.

The mission soon prospered and its harvests of corn exceeded expectations.

San Jose ranked among the largest missions. In 1824 its 1,800 people were exceeded only by the population at Mission San Luis Rey. In 1832 it was regarded as the most prosperous mission, having 12,000 cattle, 13,000 sheep, and 13,000 horses.

The last mission secularized, San Jose's property was sold in 1836. The padres remained in charge of the church itself until 1846, when the Mexican Governor Pio Pico sold the buildings for $12,000.

The facility frequently is referred to as San Jose de Guadalupe, but fathers at the mission say that the references to the Guadalupe River is a recent and historically incorrect addition to the name.

Most of the mission's buildings were destroyed in the earthquake of 1868, after which a wooden structure was built for worship. Portions of the mission, which is now a parish church, have been restored during recent years.

Mission San Jose's address is 43300 Mission Boulevard, Fremont.

RIGHT: The mission as it appears today. (Photo by the Author)

San Francisco

THE SIXTH mission founded by Father Serra was Nuestra Serafico Padre San Francisco de Asis a la Laguna de los Dolores (Our Seraphic Father St. Francis of Assisi at the Lake of Sorrows) established October 9, 1776, just a few weeks after signing of the Declaration of Independence on the other side of the continent. Some accounts give June 29 as the founding date, but Father Geiger's research indicates only that mass was said that day at the site.

The facility has popularly been called "Mission Dolores" during the years.

Captain Juan Bautista de Anza, who brought the first civilian settlers to California, selected the site. The lake helping to inspire the name later was filled.

The present mission building, started in 1782, was completed in 1791. While it does not have the arches and towers that distinguish most missions in the chain, the structure is impressive because of its simple massive lines.

The Spanish named the adjoining settlement Yerba Buena; the Americans, inspired partly by the mission but also wishing to capitalize on the port's fine facilities, changed the community's name to San Francisco.

The mission's patron is St. Francis, founder of the Franciscan order. The mission is at 16th and Dolores Streets.

This painting depicts early days at Mission San Francisco de Asis. Note the oak trees covering the surrounding hills that eventually would provide space for a major city. (California Historical Society)

ABOVE: An 1865 photo shows Mission San Francisco flanked by commercial buildings as the city boomed. (Wells Fargo Bank History Room)

RIGHT: Here is the way the mission appears today. (Redwood Empire Association)

This replica of Mission San Rafael was built in 1949 on the site of the original structure.

San Rafael

MISSION San Rafael Arcangel, 20th founded was established December 14, 1817, as an asistencia or branch of Mission San Francisco de Asis. The facility was intended as a hospital station because the damp San Francisco climate was proving too severe for the Indians.

The mission's name honors St. Raphael, the angel of bodily healing.

San Rafael's population included converts in the area north of San Francisco Bay as well as weaker Indians from San Francisco.

The buildings at San Rafael were much smaller than those at the other missions, since the station was intended only as a branch. However, the facility prospered and on October 19, 1822, was raised to full mission status.

San Rafael, secularized in 1833, was the first mission to be taken over by the Mexican government. General Mariano Vallejo, appointed official administrator, confiscated the mission's properties, including vines and fruit trees, which were replanted on private ranches. The mission buildings soon decayed into mounds of adobe mud.

The Native Sons of the Golden West erected a bell on the site in 1909 and in 1949 a replica of the mission was constructed on the approximate site of the original structures.

Mission San Rafael's address is Fifth and "A" Streets in downtown San Rafael.

ABOVE: An 1817 drawing of Mission San Rafael showed bells hanging on a framework in front of the sanctuary. (Security Pacific National Bank) BELOW: This view of the reproduced mission is from Fifth Street in downtown San Rafael.

San Francisco Solano

THE LAST and most northerly of the missions San Francisco Solano, founded July 4, 1823.

The mission, the only one started under independent Mexican rule, was established to help check the advance of Russian fur traders operating along California's northern coast.

The mission's patron (not to be confused with St. Francis of Assisi) was born in Spain in 1549 and died in Peru in 1610. He is the apostle of South America.

The founder of the mission was Padre Jose Altimire, young priest just assigned to San Francisco. He acted under direction of Governor Arguello, who in his desire to move against the Russians failed to obtain church sanction for the new mission.

The governor intended to transfer the missions at San Francisco and San Rafael to the new site. The priests protested. As a compromise, the new mission was recognized and the existing mission was permitted to continue.

In later years, it was popularly known as "Sonoma" Mission because of the pueblo founded by it in 1835.

After secularization in 1834, the mission began to decay. The present adobe church, built in 1840 to serve families in the pueblo of Sonoma, was sold in 1881 and fell into neglect after use variously as a barn, winery, and blacksmith shop.

The State of California acquired the property in 1903 and restoration of the structure was completed in 1913.

The mission at 114 East Spain Street, Sonoma, is now part of Sonoma State Historic Park.

A 1905 photograph of Mission San Francisco Solano showed the structure beginning to decay. (Security Pacific National Bank)

After its restoration in 1913, Mission San Francisco Solano became part of Sonoma State Historic Park. (California Mission Trails Association Ltd.)

Wooden pillars, instead of the adobe or brick ones associated with most missions, were used in the arcade of San Francisco Solano.

Index

(Numbers in Parentheses Indicate Illustrations)